Wanderlust

The Story of a Geordie Wanderer Extraordinaire

Tom Callaghan

Newcastle Libraries & Information Service

Front cover: Tom Callaghan in Yosemite, California, 1985 (Photo: Stuart Kandell)

Back cover: Tom with Kathy at the Cheshire Home, Ampthill, 1962.

Also by Tom Callaghan

A Lang Way To The Pawnshop
Tramp's Chronicle
Those Were The Days
At Rest Amongst The Mighty Dead

Extracts from *The Wanderlust* by Robert W. Service
are reproduced by kind permission of Feinman Krasilovsky, New York.

ISBN 1 85795 033 X

©Tom Callaghan 1997

City of Newcastle upon Tyne,
Community & Leisure Services Department,
Newcastle Libraries & Information Service, 1997

Cataloguing-in-Publication Data: A catalogue record for this book is available from the British Library.

Printed by Athenaeum Press, Team Valley, Gateshead.

CONTENTS   Page

In dedication
to
Kathleen Peggy Walton
who shared many of the adventures
related in this book.

Highway, by-way, many a mile I've done;
Rare way, fair way, many a height I've won;
But I'm pulling my freight in the morning boys,
And it's over the hills or bust!
For there's never a cure
When you list to the lure
        Of the Wan-der-lust.

The Wanderlust, Robert W. Service

I must confess I hold no nursing certificates! What remarks I have made on Life
in those Caring Institutions I was employed in, are solely based on experience,
common sense, and compassion.

Tom Callaghan

Institutional Insanity

It was an afternoon in early January, 1944; I had entered the reading room of the public library in order to scan the vacancy columns of the local paper, but had got into conversation with Little Franky, a well-known local character who held court in the Bigg Market every Sunday evening. During the winter months, the library reading room was a kind of club to men like Franky who had no fixed abode; it was warm and comfortable. Mind you, Little Franky was not the kind of common lodging house acquaintance who used the reading room as a place to sleep his time away. He went there to study, to furnish his mind with material for all the tall stories he spun in the Bigg Market in order to earn a few shillings. Whatever tales he told, one could rest assured that Franky had read up all the details and dates to fit the story he would be relating at that particular time: Mouthpiece for Al Capone; A Spy during the First World War; Personal Bodyguard to Winston Churchill; Explorer Extraordinary; etc. With his diminutive wiry figure, and that permanent mischievous glimmer in his eyes, he reminded me of one of those leprechauns my grandmother had told me about when I was a lad.

We were discussing the war, and the problems it had created, when suddenly Franky remarked, "By god, Tom, I'm dying of thirst."

Of course he was aware I was at present employed as a cinema doorman and likely to have a few shillings on me. I wasn't surprised at the tap, I had expected it.

"Don't die here, Franky," I responded, "I don't wish to be implicated in your sudden demise." I extracted a florin from my jacket pocket and passed it over to Franky, who appeared delighted at the sight of the two-shilling coin.

"You've saved my life, pal," said he, thanking me briskly before departing on his way to the nearest pub. As soon as he had gone I got the opportunity to consult the *Evening Chronicle* and I began scanning the vacancy columns! I had lost count of the jobs I'd had since leaving the compulsive Elementary Education System; being instructed crude Mythology as the word of God; and Tyranny described as History, and other nonsensical subjects totally unrelated to future means of wage-earning. I was now in my second job since being discharged from the Royal Navy, with a perforated ear drum – a cinema doorman! By Jove, Thomas, some future there.

One particular vacancy held my attention: "Male Student Nurses required at a Mental Hospital in Kent". Here was the chance to enter a profession – and work that I had always been curious about. It recalled to my mind two quaint characters who had lived in my neighbourhood when I was a lad. Both of them had spent some time in Coxlodge, the City Asylum. They were inoffensive men, but because it was known they had been patients in the lunatic asylum, they were the constant victims of some of the local children who thoughtlessly tormented them. Among the adults, there were those who gave them wide berth, whilst others patronised them as though they were backward children. I remembered a Sunday afternoon I had walked over the Town Moor and on to Coxlodge, and made a complete circuit of the asylum walls, which took me some time despite being a swift walker. This convinced me that the colony must be a huge place. On my way home I had wondered what life was like for the inmates existing behind those High Walls.

The next day I sent off my application. To my delight I was successful. I now had the opportunity to enter a real profession, and to prove to myself that my continuous job-drifting since leaving school was at an end. So I began serving my notice at the cinema. What I required now was a suitcase in which to lodge my few personal possessions. Being unable to afford a new one, I paid a visit to my Aunt Dolly, who had a secondhand shop on Scotswood Road, that lang lang road that led to Blaydon. My aunt appeared amused on learning the nature of my new job.

"Well, bonny lad, I haven't a suitcase on the premises; but we'll have a cup of tea before you go. Mary! Put the kettle on dear," she called out to her daughter, who was in the kitchen at the rear of the shop. "What on earth made you decide to go in for nursing in a mental hospital of all places, Thomas?" she inquired.

"I wanted to be a doctor when I was a lad, Aunty; I couldn't afford to, so training to become a nurse is the next best thing," I replied.

"You wanted to be so many things when you were a lad, Thomas: A blacksmith; then a singer; an actor; a writer; you're a romantic grasshopper, bonny lad," retorted she as my cousin came down the steps from the kitchen carrying a tray with three mugs of tea on it.

"Mary dear, your cousin Thomas has got himself a new job; this time in a lunatic asylum, down London or thereabouts. You better kiss him goodbye, you may never see him again," said my aunt, laughing good humouredly.

"I'll give him six months at the most, mother, and he'll be back in Newcastle looking for another job," remarked Mary, teasingly.

"I'll prove you wrong, Mary, and me Dad too. I'll remain in this job until I retire. I'll find myself a wife and settle down," said I earnestly.

"It's time you were married, bonny lad; you've had as many girlfriends as you've had jobs. But I think she'll be a clever girl whoever gets you to church, or the Registry Office," said my aunt.

"Goodness me, I'm only twenty years old, Aunt; too young for marriage, and too hard-up," I said.

Kissing them both I left the shop. My visits to the other secondhand shops on the road were in vain.

On a Monday morning I left home with my few belongings secured in brown pawnshop paper and string. On arriving at Kings Cross, and on the advice of some spiv-like character who claimed to know the geography of the underground railway, like the back of his well-manicured hands, I descended below, and suffered the most complicated journey of my life, before finally ascending at the Strand. At Charing Cross, I boarded my final train, and so arrived at Bexley!

✳✳✳

The length of the hospital driveway and the obvious extent of the grounds convinced me that a small township could have been built inside them. In the reception hall directly under the clocktower I was introduced to one of the deputy chief male nurses. First giving my parcel a brief curious glance, he led me down seemingly endless corridors to the deputy chief's office. After a few minutes discussion, he then presented me with a copy of the nurse's rule book, and a lanyard having two large keys and a whistle attached to it. We then left the office, walked along more corridors, through an airing-court, an orchard, and finally on to a driveway which led away from the main hospital towards an L-shaped villa in the distance, which as the deputy informed me was the male tubercular clinic ward, and where I was to be billeted. This information made me feel a little uneasy, but on being shown over my bedsitter I felt fine. In all my twenty years, I had never been blessed with the luxurious comforts that were being offered to me now. A room to myself, a bed to myself, furniture of my own including a large wardrobe – despite having little or nothing to place inside it. In the grate a fire was blazing in all its glory – and a big scuttle of coal nearby; no signs of coal shortage here – even the devil himself would have rejoiced at the sight.

After the deputy had left, a tall well-built patient introduced himself, informing me that he had been responsible for the comfortable appearance of my room, and would I care to engage him as my batman, wage, half-a-crown a week. I engaged him there and then.

Later that evening on returning from the dining room, the night-nurse informed me he was a native of Jarrow, so we were on the same wavelength immediately, and I sat down at his desk to have a chat after he had completed his task of serving out the nightly Paraldehyde cocktails, the smell of which was sufficient to overcome any sensitive person; and I supposed being on duty alone, looking after thirty-six patients, such obnoxious draughts might be considered necessary. During our conversation I suddenly observed a patient who was sitting up in bed in the middle of the ward turn round to face the wall – and carry out some odd manoeuvre towards what appeared to be from where I was sitting, an electric wall-point completing this act he then apparently placed some object under his pillow, then once more resumed gazing in our direction! The nurse, observing my curiosity, explained.

"When you're on night duty, Tom, you have to keep pegging that wall-point every hour, to prove to the superintendent, that you're alert. Old Gabby there, he's a night-bird, he sleeps most of the day so he volunteers to clock-in for me; that's why I've got the desk-lamp beaming on to the wall clock facing his bed, so he can see when it's time to use the key. I keep him going in sweets, and of course he likes to think he's doing something useful, poor fellow."

"How do the patients contract TB in this place?" I asked.

"Well, no doubt some of the poor devils would have arrived here suffering from the disease, and of course being placed on over-crowded wards in the main hospital, they most probably infected a few more patients before being discovered as carriers."

"How about those out there on the verandah, are they the worst cases?" I inquired further.

"Yes. When you come on duty on this ward, which you're bound to some day, always wear a mask when you're shaving any of them. We get a patient to wash out the sputum mugs," he confided in me.

After a mug of tea with him, I bid him goodnight. "By the way, will you give me a call at six, in the morning, please, I'm on early shift," said I.

"Of course I will Tom, goodnight son," he replied.

On undressing I put out the light, then opened my window, which I discovered was blocked so as to allow it to open top or bottom by no more than four inches. Within minutes of lying in my most comfortable bed I felt myself falling off to sleep. And just at the point when I was about to float off into dreamland I was violently alerted by piercing screams, the kind of disturbing sounds that any individual would associate only with the insane asylum. Springing out of bed and putting on my trousers I grabbed hold of my lanyard and peered out into the ward, just in time to observe the nurse coming out of one of the siderooms holding a small kidney dish containing an hypodermic syringe.

"Sorry about that, Geordie; he's often like this, poor fellow. I've given him an injection, so you won't be troubled any more tonight."

✳✳✳

Next morning, by trial and error, I again found my way to the male staff dining room situated in the main hospital. I was certainly impressed with the layout of this huge Victorian-built institution. I thought it would take a clever inmate to escape from its confines; they would need to possess wings to fly over the high perimeter walls. In the dining room I was joined at the table by an Irishman, Michael O'Sullevan, who informed me I was commencing duty on his ward. I observed he didn't appear to have much of an early-morning appetite.

"They're a nice bunch of fellows to work with, Tom," said he, admiring the way I was stoking the grub inside me. "And the patients are not a rough lot. There are one or two crafty buggers, but you'll soon get to know them."

After breakfast we made our way to K. Ward. On arrival Mike pressed a bell-push situated on the wall to the left of the door before inserting the key into the lock, winking wisely at me as he did so. "Always ring the bell before you enter any ward, Tom, the staff then know that it is one of the nurses on his way in, and not one of the Chiefs, or the Doctor."

Once inside the ward corridor he slammed the self-locking door behind him. On both sides of the corridor were a number of siderooms, all of which I observed, contained a bed and a locker. These rooms I learned were allotted to the workers who grafted at various tasks in the hospital. At the top of the corridor on the right was a dormitory containing forty beds close together. To the left was the dining room – which really was an adjunct to the dayroom. Facing the tables and on the left, were the ward kitchen, two padded cells, an ordinary sideroom, and ward office. At the far end of the dayroom, leading off to the left, was the Infirmary ward holding twenty beds. The door leading out to the airing-court was situated on the right of the dayroom and almost facing the entrance to that of the infirmary.

I followed O'Sullevan into the staff room where we removed our jackets and put on white coats, then he led me to the ward office and introduced me to the Charge Nurse and other staff. After a brief exchange of greetings, I was detailed to work along with Mike at bed-making. In the dormitory six patients were busy, but they ceased their activity to scan me.

"Are you the new nurse, sir?" inquired three of them in unison.

"I can't understand anyone coming all the way from Newcastle to work in this bloody silly place," remarked a fourth patient, dryly.

"All right, that's enough, bugger off all of you," remarked Mike, who then delegated the dry character to work alongside me. Within five minutes he was finding fault with my every move, and of course his deliberate disruptive tactics soon resulted in our remaining at one particular bed too long for the liking of Mike, who apparently had been silently observing him, and just as quietly he approached behind and gently kicked him in the pants.

"Now then, Jarvis, let me tell you that Nurse Callaghan is here to tell you what to do, and not you to tell him!"

"I was only showing him the proper way to make beds," interjected Jarvis, displaying some show of defiance.

"Would you like to go to bed for the rest of the day?" retorted Michael. The patient appeared visibly alarmed.

"No sir. I was only..."

O'Sullevan cut him short: "Make beds, and hold your tongue" said he firmly.

In no time at all we were ahead of the others; it was obvious to me that the threat of being sent to bed – and without breakfast – had motivated the rebel to action and not words. Indeed the warning must have impressed the other five patients for by the time the call for breakfast was heard, all of the beds in the dormitory were made.

Whilst the other staff served out the meal, a deputy Charge Nurse directed me to take a plate of sausage sandwiches and a mug of tea in to the patient in No. 1 padded cell, and remain with him until he had completed his breakfast. As I entered, the patient, with a few days growth on his face, and clothed only in a thick canvas shirt, sprang up from off the canvas sheet he had been sitting on and eagerly relieved me of the plate and mug, thanking me as he did so, though I detected his slight irritation at my presence as he ate; and naturally I felt a little embarrassed at having to remain.

On returning to the ward kitchen with the utensils, the same nurse told me to go into the sideroom next to the office and collect a tin basin, dessert spoon and tin mug. The patient who was sitting up in bed appeared to be a large man. I could not see any signs of the items I had come to collect, so I asked him whether any other nurse had been and removed them. He just smiled at me as though I was a simpleton. I peered under the bed, in the commode, then finally turned back the bedding, to discover the basin and mug, but of the desert spoon, only a portion of the stem. I formed the instant opinion that I had been detailed to observe the wrong patient.

This was the character I ought to have been keeping an eye on while he breakfasted. I reported the fact – the bed was stripped but in vain. O'Sullevan and myself were sent outside to search the area beneath the window – nothing! It was now obvious the patient concerned had achieved the almost impossible by swallowing the best part of a dessert spoon; a feat equal to the performance of any ostrich. I reckoned it would take a number of large doses of liquid paraffin to relieve him of the hardware.

Breakfast over, Mike and I, set up the barber's shop in the bathroom. I soon discovered to my dismay that each safety blade was supposed to perform a dozen shaves or more, and considering the patients were only shaved every two days, each grimace of theirs had my deepest sympathy! I couldn't help thinking at the time of all the countless tons of steel being used at that moment for the useless purpose of war, and we having to risk committing carnages on the faces of these unfortunate men all for the want of a few extra penny blades.

At ten o'clock, we went into the ward kitchen to have our morning break – sausages borrowed from the patients' rations. Mike, who had eaten almost nothing in the staff dining room earlier that morning, proved he did have an appetite after all; I continued to prove I had a far better one.

On completing my break, I was detailed to relieve the other junior nurse in the infirmary. Fourteen of the twenty beds were occupied. The Staff Nurse, who was also a qualified SRN in general nursing, was busy attending to the dressings; my task was to hand him whatever he required from the trolley. The patient he was attending to at that moment, on recognising I was a stranger, immediately began telling me his tales of woe. He informed me he was an American, and an inventor, one of his inventions being the first telescopic umbrella which unfortunately had been stolen from him by a fellow countryman and patented. I had no means then to assess whether his claims were genuine, or the result of his fancies. The Staff Nurse said nothing but just continued with cleansing the angry-looking wound on the patient's buttock; the red-raw cavity was a vicious sight, and I was amazed at the fortitude displayed by the patient.

When the other junior nurse returned from his break, I returned to the bathroom to assist O'Sullevan at shaving. As before, Mike had posted a particular patient in the bathroom door facing the passageway that led directly into the dining room, to act as a scout!

"The doctor has just gone by," remarked the scout suddenly. I was at the moment attempting to stem the bleeding of a patient's chin which I had nicked.

"Will he come in here?" I asked Mike.

"The doctor? No, no danger of that," he replied. "He'll sign the ward report-book, the medicine cards, glance in the dayroom, and vanish for the rest of the day."

He informed me that due to the war there was a shortage of doctors, and as every ward had to be visited daily, that exercise alone took up his duty time. At 11.30, we closed up shop for the morning; those left unshaved would suffer their scrape at the hands of the afternoon shift. After returning the shaving tackle to the office, I went along to the ward kitchen. Michael, for some reason was reprimanding the worker who had just arrived from the main kitchen with the food trolley:

"All right, Charlie, another word from you, and off to bed you'll go for the rest of the day." The threat worked wonders!

While we were unloading the trolley, one of the Charge Nurses entered the kitchen. Carving a chunk off the pork joint, he placed it on a plate and put it in the cupboard; the staff's afternoon tea was now provided for. When the patients were all served in the dining room, I was directed to take a lunch into the padded cell for Baines. As at breakfast time, he reminded me of a child who is locked away from the rest of the family for having acted a little unruly. After he had completed his meal, I was about to secure the inner door of the pad, when the Charge Nurse called out to me to leave it open and accompany him to the clothing store. He handed me a bundle of clothing along with a black pair of leather slippers: "Take those to Baines, tell him to dress, then take him into the dayroom."

When I entered the cell with his clothes his eyes lit up with eagerness, and he dressed swiftly. I was not aware at that moment how long he had been incarcerated inside his gloomy sound-proof cell, but I felt sure no long-term prisoner could have expressed more joy and relief on being released from his prison. On entering the dayroom the Charge Nurse provided him with a cigarette and a light – he had obviously been gasping for a smoke.

By one o'clock the dining room was clear; I was off duty at two, so until then I was told to sit in the dayroom with O'Sullevan, to keep observation on the patients. Due to my being a stranger in their midst, I soon realised that the observation exercise was a two-way affair, for the wide boys were seriously taking stock of me also. My first impression of the dayroom atmosphere reminded me of my school days; if some individual rose from his chair, perhaps only to stretch his legs, or look around the room, he was instantly and abruptly ordered to sit down, by Mike. Whether he was doing so solely to impress me I couldn't tell but I had never up to that moment set eyes upon such a pathetic and apparently subdued collection of human beings in my life; not even the pitiful sights I had once witnessed in the office of my local Board of Guardians, when I was a boy, could compare with this scene in this mental hospital dayroom.

As I was going off duty, one of the ward-workers was lounging around in the corridor leading to the ward exit, and he asked me to post him a letter. He was handing it to me, along with the money for the postage, when Michael arrived on the scene:

"Now then, Jackson," he called out sternly, "you know the rules! Take that letter to the ward office and hand it in to the Charge Nurse. And don't try that again."

On the way to the staff dining room, Mike advised me: "Never accept mail from any patient, Tom. You see, their letters are censored before they go out; when you have been here a while, you will see the sense in it."

After lunch I returned to my room. My batman was waiting for me in order to make my bed, light my fire and stock me up in coal.

"Do you know what the deputy chief male nurse said to me this morning, sir?" he remarked as he was building the fire.

"I haven't a clue, Sergeant," I replied, addressing him in the manner he was accustomed to.

"He said I'm a German spy. I'm not a spy, sir, I'm too busy to spy. I'm working all day on the ward, polishing floors, washing dishes, and making beds; then when I return to my own ward at teatime, I have to work there. He has no right to call me a spy, has he, sir."

"Don't worry about it," I replied consolingly, "he's probably jealous of all the medals on your chest," said I, in reference to all the nondescript badges on both lapels of his jacket.

After tea on the Tuesday of my second week, I was detailed along with O'Sullevan to escort the dance party to the main hall where the weekly dance was held. The fourteen fortunate patients, all of them workers, either employed on the ward, the farm or gardens, were busy sprucing themselves for the occasion.

The few who possessed private clothes for such times appeared pretty smart, but the others, in their drab institutional rig which bore the stamp of the workhouse pauperism, looked pathetic. We took off our white coats and donned our jackets. On the way to the hall, Mike told me to keep my eyes peeled to ensure that none of the patients got up to any hanky-panky whilst dancing, and that none of them passed any notes to their partners.

The seating arrangements in the all were strictly segregated: male patients in rows the length of one side of the hall, the females facing them from the opposite side. The music was provided by gramophone records; and in charge of the machine were the male and female Charge Nurses on rota duty. The first record, a Strauss

Waltz, no sooner began playing than the majority of men and women sprang to their feet and swiftly advanced towards each other, their arms raised and apart, a hungry awareness displayed on their faces. It became instantly obvious to me that most of the patients had their own special partners, and possessiveness was acute. Quite a number of the men could no more dance than fly, yet they appeared to be enjoying themselves solely by holding in their arms someone of the opposite sex and shuffling around the floor with them! Suddenly a pretty young lady crossed the floor and made straight to where I was sitting.

"Hello love. Would you care to dance?" she asked me, after first winking cutely to Michael.

"Now then, Sadie," began Mike, smiling broadly, "you know staff are not supposed to dance, not even with beautiful colleens like yourself. Though I'm sure Nurse Callaghan here would only be too please to oblige you. Wait until he becomes a Charge Nurse then he'll have more leeway."

Sadie appeared surprised to learn that I was on the staff; no doubt because I was not in uniform.

"I'm sorry love. I thought you were a new patient; and a good-looking one at that," she replied, smiling impishly.

"Don't apologise my dear," I responded. "I'm flattered that you should bother to single me out from a crowd."

A female nurse approached Sadie, a faint trace of a smile upon her lips: "Come on Sadie, what are you after over here all this time? Either choose a partner and dance – or go back to your own side of the hall and sit down."

Sadie looked defiantly at the nurse. "I was only asking this young man if he wished to dance; I didn't know he was a nurse," she retorted.

"Well you know now dear; he can't dance with you when he's on duty, you know that," replied the nurse.

"Nor any other bloody time according to the rules of this place – Goodbye love, for now," she smiled at me, then stalked away towards the other side of the hall, swaying her shapely hips provocatively, the nurse following behind her.

"I will say this about Sadie, she's very selective, and picks out all the young good-looking men," remarked Mike, grinning. "And I think Kathleen has her eyes on you too," he added.

"They call the nurse Kathleen, do they?" said I, observing her crossing the floor. "I wouldn't mind being introduced to her, Mike."

"I'll pass the word on, Tom" promised Mike, smiling broadly.

A few minutes later, Mike rose and went onto the floor and began manoeuvring among the dancers, deliberately creating the impression he was indulging in a little horse-play; in fact he had observed two of the couples passing notes to each other; so had I, but it was my intention to ignore the patients' bush-telegram system if at all possible. When he returned he sat down next to me and discreetly read the notes, then passed them on to me, so as I could slip into the toilet and flush them away. They were harmless sentimental love notes; yet I was aware that if Mike had reported the patients concerned in the transactions, they would have been returned to their respective wards at once, and suffered the penalty of having their privileges withdrawn; such as they were. Finally the last dance came to an end; it was a quick hug and a snap kiss between each couple, then time to escort them back to the wards, and segregation. Back on K ward, the returning patients were given their cocoa, then off to bed. The majority of the other patients were already in bed; bedtime was 6.30 p.m., winter or summer.

※※※

It was a Sunday, breakfast just completed and the patients still sitting at table, waiting for the daily routine of pill distribution. The Staff Nurse came with the medicine tray, beginning his task at the first table near the office. "Open your mouth!" was the demand. A capsule, or a tablet, was placed on the patient's tongue, then "Swallow it." Most of the patients obliged instantly for they were so accustomed to doing as they were told. But there were individuals who had to be encouraged a little: tablet or capsule forced into the mouth, then lips and chin clasped manually; it was useless struggling, so in despair and defeat they would swallow the tranquilliser – if only for the relief of being able to breathe freely again.

On the medicine tray there appeared to be drugs to suit all types of mental distress; for a few hours, perhaps their mental strife would subside; and there is no doubt that the distribution of the drugs assisted the staff in dealing with an overcrowded ward, for without them there would probably be more aggression between a number of particular patients; boredom, alone, would promote it!

At half-past-nine, the Charge Nurse rounded up eight C of E patients and detailed me to accompany them to church. Many more would have liked to go along with me, but I don't think the Charge liked to boost the Chaplain's ego all that much.

Back on the ward, and after the coffee-break, Mike and I, and one of the deputy Charges, took the patients out into the airing court. A few minutes past eleven o'clock the air-raid sirens sounded, followed soon after by anti-aircraft gunfire, then the approach of a flying-bomb could be heard. Its engine, sounding similar to that of a motor cycle, suddenly cut out right overhead. The three of us began calling out to the patients to lie flat on the ground, for it was known that once the engine of a flying-bomb cut out, it either descended directly down, or it glided for some distance. This particular one glided, and came down and exploded on some nearby farmland. While we were down, a patient named Simpson had taken it into his head to take advantage of the confusion and make a reckless bid for freedom. It was only on regaining our feet that another patient called out that Simpson had managed to clear the six-foot railings that surrounded the airing court. By the time Mike and I had gone through the wicket gate, Simpson was sprinting off in the direction of the farm, towards the perimeter wall. Mike sounded a number of short blasts on his whistle, which rapidly brought out another three male nurses from adjoining courts, and the five of us fanned out and began chasing the absconder who by now was almost out of sight. We closed in just as Simpson was attempting the awkward task of scaling the high wall. After a brief struggle he let go his hold; though his face was flushed with the unusual exertion, that factor could not conceal the deep disappointment he was feeling and he was visibly attempting to hold back the tears that were beginning to ooze from his sad eyes. One of the nurses smacked him over the head, another made to follow suit, but Mike intercepted the intended blow: "Let him be, Harry, he's buggered out."

The Charge Nurse was writing some details in the report book when we entered the ward office. Laying down his pen, he glanced up at Simpson, an ironical smile upon his face, and spoke:

"Where were you intending going in such a hurry, Simpson?"

"To my sister's in Finchley, sir," replied he meekly.

"Then why don't you leave in a proper manner if you wish to go to your sister's?" asked the Charge Nurse, teasingly. "You only have to ask, and I will open the door for you." Simpson cast his eyes down on to his shoes to evade the fixed gaze of his tormentor.

"Take him away and put him in the empty sideroom," said the Charge. "See that he undresses and gets into bed. And give him no lunch, I'm sure he's too worn out to eat anything now."

The following morning, Monday was general bath day! Although there were two large baths in the bathroom on the ward, only a small number of the patients were ever bathed in them, usually the ward workers, and the odd patient who might be confined in one of the special siderooms. The majority of the patients were escorted to the general bathroom situated outside the ward on the corridor. On such days, by now, I was often detailed to attend to the patients' feet, having proved that I was good at removing corns and callouses. Years later, and after much experience, I was to attempt to earn my living as a chiropodist.

At the beginning, I had wondered how so many patients could be suffering from corns and callouses, considering the number of years that the majority of them had been incarcerated and accustomed to remaining almost immobile all day and every day. Later I was to learn that the reason was quite simple – poverty, which had resulted in their having had to wear ill-fitting secondhand footwear almost from the day they had learned to walk.

I never saw men who relished and enjoyed the opportunity of being able to stand under a warm shower as these poor mortals did; if given the chance, many of them would have remained under the shower for an hour or more, if for no other reason than to escape from the confines of the dayroom! Indeed there were patients who quite willingly took to scrubbing floors, and polishing, or working elsewhere in the hospital, or in the grounds, as a relief from sitting all day like dummies in the day-room. It was one fact I had observed from my early days in the hospital, that most of the manual labour in the colony was performed by the patients. In return, most of them received a few cigarettes or sweets weekly; those few who possessed a parole-card which enabled them to go outside the confines of the hospital received a little pocket-money. As far as I could make out, the therapeutic value of such work was a sham, it was the economic value of the inmates' labour towards the upkeep of the colony which counted. Those who were able to work yet refused, simply had their privileges withdrawn; this penalty was always effective. It was Workhouse Economic Philosophy.

Of course, there were individuals who really liked to be working, it was part of their nature. One particular patient in this group who ironically was named 'Idle' was a compulsive worker. His mental condition seemed to make him search out tasks to perform. He would have scrubbed all the many corridors in the hospital daily if given the opportunity. Indeed he had to be sedated every night for there was no other way to keep him in bed – and so off to sleep; despite this he was the first to rise on a morning, completely unaffected by the nightly dose of Paraldehyde. He appeared to exist to eat, drink tea, work – and more work, and smoke his pipe. Anyone, other than staff, who attempted to engage him in conversation received abuse for their bother, usually "Bugger off". Furthermore they had better keep their cranium out of reach of his scrubbing brush or else they would feel the weight of it on their skulls. He was a complete loner. His abrupt behaviour was tolerated by the staff for he was such a valued worker.

I certainly couldn't complain of my lot, the three months I had been working in the colony was for me as good as being resident in Shangri-La! There were extensive grounds to stroll around and I loved walking in a country environment. There were books to borrow, a cinema / dance hall, a church if I felt like attending. I could even have a haircut, and have my shoes repaired providing I was discreet about it; and I was receiving rations which would have been hard to come by if I lived outside the hospital, in the wartime ration-book society. Besides, I had been befriended by one of the deputy Charge Nurses and his wife, who were ever so kind to me; inviting me to their home; even presenting me with new shirts and pyjamas purchased from their local Co-op Stores; all I contributed were the clothing coupons. I had never received such kindness before. And of course by now I was courting Kathleen. I was determined to lower my anchor, and take roots.

By time the bathing was over, it was near midday, and the tables were being laid for lunch. After the meal, and before the patients rose from the table, the cutlery was counted; the usual procedure; it was discovered that a knife was missing on one particular table. After a search it was found in the trouser pocket of a patient called Wilson. He was taken into the bathroom and interrogated, though without much response at first.

"Don't act so dumb or stupid, Wilson, you're not as simple as you make out to be," called out the Charge Nurse, who was becoming annoyed by the lack of co-operation from the patient. Finally Wilson was stripped, and dumped into a bath of cold water, his head forcibly submerged until he called out wildly: confessing he intended using the knife to prise the lock of the ward exit door so as he could go for a walk in the grounds! That admission alone proved to me the state of the poor fellow's mind; it would in my estimation have taken a battering ram to dislodge the lock on any of the stout secure doors in the hospital in the absence of a master key. One thing was certain, to be forcibly submerged in a very cold bath immediately after a meal would not do his nervous system any good; it was just as well he was confined to bed as a further punishment.

※※※

Visiting time was of vital importance as far as the patients were concerned, for the weekly visit was their only contact with that other life of so long ago. I had learned that there were numerous patients who were never visited; the main reason being either that their immediate next-of-kin, or friends, had passed on; or perhaps were too old to continue with visits; as a result these patients tended to retire more into themselves. Those patients who did get visits appeared to sit in the dayroom with their visitors, spending what little time there was being fed with confectionery tit-bits, until it seemed they would burst apart. All their family and friends must have pooled their ration coupons in order to produce such unusual abundance of biscuits and sweets in order that the patients concerned could make gluttons of themselves!

One particular visiting afternoon I was sitting in the ward kitchen so as to be near the exit in order to answer the door bell. On one of my journeys down the corridor to open the door I observed Bloodworth, standing outside one of the side-rooms, occupied in ripping his jacket to shreds, having already made a mess of his shirt! He was one of the few patients on the ward who was supposed to be kept under strict observation, on account of his insatiable urge to tear his clothing, curtains, or anything else that could be torn apart. I wondered whether my two colleagues in the dayroom were asleep. After admitting the visitors, I escorted Bloodworth to the ward office.

"Do you want any clippings for mat-making, sir?" I asked the senior Charge.

He glanced at Bloodworth, in his usual dry fashion: "You'll never get any visitors, John, if you keep tearing your clothes to bits; you cost more to keep than anyone else on the ward. Take him into the infirmary ward and tell the Staff Nurse to put him in the top bed near the sluice. He's going to have an operation tomorrow!"

After the visitors had left, the Staff Nurse set to work on Bloodworth's head, first with the shears, then a razor, until it resembled a large billiard ball.

"You seem to be preparing him for the Electric Chair," I commented jokingly. He then informed me that an American surgical team were arriving the following day and were going to perform a leucotomy on the patient.

"What is a leucotomy, then?" I asked.

"It's brain surgery," he replied, without going into details.

"I wonder if the Charge Nurse would allow me to go to the operating theatre tomorrow," I inquired.

"Well I need someone with me, so if you're keen about it I'll speak to him for you, I'm sure he'll agree," he replied.

At five-thirty, that same afternoon, I was detailed for relief duty on H ward. I left by way of the dayroom and through the airing court to the next block, and reported to the Charge in his office; he was another dry character:

"Welcome to the Lions' den, Geordie," said he, greeting me with a faint trace of a smile. "Let me warn you, if you fall asleep on this ward, you do so at your own risk because they're all mad on this one. By the way, I hear you're courting an Irish nurse! Well with a name like yours you ought to be welcome in to her parlour. Right son, pop in the dayroom and relieve Nurse Bailey."

When Bailey left I occupied his armchair. There were two other nurses present. I had no sooner sat down than I observed that a number of patients appeared to be developing hallucinatory ideas about my sudden appearance among them. And it did not take long for their fierce-looking grimaces to convince me, and warn me, that to them their delusions were real; so I had better accept that, or watch out! A while later one of the other nurses lit a cigarette. Instantly numerous pairs of eyes focused longingly upon him, or rather on his cigarette; then in turn, they eyed each other – the kind of scrutiny which could only mean "anyone who attempts to leave his seat and prepares to move in the direction of the smoker had better look out!" On smoking his cigarette down to the butt, the nurse with a flick of the finger sent it into the middle of the dayroom floor, and instantly about seven patients sprang from their seats and pounced upon the fag-end, as though they were a pack of starving dogs after a juicy bone. As in all dog-fights the roughest participant retrieved the remains of the tobacco, which he rolled up inside a slip of toilet paper, then begged the same nurse to provide him with a light!

I thought it was a silly means of distraction, or amusement, for I was aware that on this particular ward there were sufficient skirmishes among the patients without any of the staff, however unwittingly, adding to them.

By six-thirty, they all had finished drinking their cocoa, and minutes later they were all undressed, their clothes and slippers all bundled up and placed on one of the tables in the dining room; this reminded me of the pawnshop I used to visit when I was a lad, so neat were the bundles of clothing.

The following afternoon on reporting for duty on my own ward, the Charge Nurse detailed me to assist the Staff Nurse, and accompany Bloodworth to the operating theatre. Once we had placed the patient in the hands of the anaesthetists, we went into the changing room and donned theatre dress. This was my first time ever inside an operating theatre; I glanced around, especially at the varied array of surgical instruments laid out for use, with a mixture of interest, and alarm. Once we had placed the patient on the operating table, one of the surgical team, removed the dressing from the patient's head and swabbed the cranium carefully. Then stepping aside for the next surgeon, who was obviously the team leader, to take over, he was handed a scalpel by the Staff Nurse. After a few muffled words to his two colleagues, he made a circular incision on each side of the head, clipping back the flesh as he did so. After further swabbing, he was handed a burr, complete with burr-end; this instrument resembled a silver-finished brace-and-bit. To my amazement, he then bored a small hole through each side of the skull. After a brief discussion with his colleagues, he nodded to the Staff Nurse, who then handed him silver-clip forceps; with these, he carefully severed a particular brain fibre in both sides of the skull. After more swabbing, and further discussion, the head surgeon stepped aside and allowed another member of the team to take over and stitch the wounds. In the recovery room, whist the team worked on Bloodworth to bring him round, they chatted to the Staff Nurse and myself quite freely; there was no sign of stuffiness about these American gentlemen. From the talk I learned about the nature of the operation, which was an irreversible one, but not the reason why it had been performed upon this particular patient.

Within a week of the operation, Bloodworth was being encouraged out of bed for a time each day. The operation must have been successful from a medical point of view for there appeared to be no adverse physical effects. As time passed it dawned upon me there was one remarkable change in the behaviour of Bloodworth – he had lost the urge to destroy his clothing, or anything else he used to tear up indiscriminately before the operation. Whatever the reason for the leucotomy, this destructive behaviour pattern had been eradicated.

I had just returned to my room from a walk around the grounds, when someone knocked on my door; and I heard O'Sullevan calling out: "Has anyone seen that Geordie hermit?" I opened the door:

"Come on in, Michael, sit down – Now then, let me attempt to analyse your motives for calling on me ..."

O'Sullevan burst out laughing; his was a kind of infectious mirth, it did one good just to listen to the deep musical sound of it, and one couldn't help joining in.

"Tom, me boy. Prove to me that you are a good psychoanalyst. What did I come here seeking you for?" asked Mike.

"It's elementary, my dear O'Sullevan. Our last meal was fish and chips, which undoubtedly has resulted in a huge thirst, and you intend going to where you can quench it. So you're here to inquire whether I will accompany you to the tavern."

"You know Tom, someday in the future, the disciples of Freud will seek to worship at your feet. So make sure they are clean." And once more he broke out in laughter.

Walking over the heath towards the pub, Mike decided to examine some of his rabbit snares; he had them placed all over the heath. In the first trap we came to, and lying there exhausted to the point of death, was a plump rabbit, its hind legs firmly caught in the trap. Its little eyes, so weak, appeared to be curtained by a film of tears, and no longer seemed to be portraying the obvious hours of agony it must have suffered. On the contrary, they gave me the impression they were revealing acute sadness, as though inquiring of us How could you be so cruel to such a small creature as I? Extricating the animal, Mike was about to conceal it in the undergrowth intending to collect it on the way back, when I reminded him that it was still alive. Seeking a large stone, Mike soon separated the poor creature from what little breath it had left in it.

Arriving at the pub, I suggested we remain in the garden, it being a warm night, and he went inside the bar to return with two pints of beer. It tasted to me like wine, so fresh it was; Mike, who had no imagination, claimed his tasted like beer. We drained our second pint when we heard the sound of the piano being played in the saloon, Mike decided to go inside. On entering, we observed Kathleen, and Mike's girlfriend Margaret, along with a group of other nurses. They were in the company of a number of soldiers from the nearby camp. On being served, we strolled over towards them, and were greeted by our respective girlfriends; but as far as the soldiers were concerned it was apparent that O'Sullevan and I were interlopers.

Kathleen and I left the pub before Mike and Margaret. Walking over the heath, I suggested to her that we dismantle all of Mike's rabbit snares.

"But surely Michael is your friend," she replied, looking surprised.

"He is my dear, that is why I'm after saving his soul! You see, he is a very inefficient executioner; half of the rabbits that stray into his traps die a slow agonising death. It's a poor pastime for a nurse." Just at that moment Michael and Margaret caught up with us.

"Ah! Michael!" began Kathleen eagerly. "Thomas and I, have been discussing how to save your soul."

A huge grin appeared on his faced as he glanced at each of us in turn. "Have either of you thought of a way?" he asked.

"It is really left to yourself," continued Kathleen. "To begin with stop slaughtering little bunny rabbits."

Michael laughed so much that he broke out in a fit of coughing. On recovering, he replied, "Oh my goodness, Kathleen, you'll slaughter me if you come out with any more jokes like that one. You ought to take no notice of Thomas here. I'm sure if he had his way he would release about two-thirds of the patients in the hospital, for he claims that number, in his opinion, were never insane in the first place. Is that right, Thomas?" asked Mike.

"That is my opinion, Mike" I replied.

"So there you are, Kathleen my love," went on Mike. "We are in the company of a man who will make most of us unemployed if he ever becomes, Medical Superintendent. Now then, Kathleen, about bunny rabbits; they are of no consequence whatever in this world, apart from enjoying them in a pie. I never give them a thought. How about a song, Tom. 'Run rabbit run'!", and once more he broke out in laughter.

"Margaret, take Michael away with you," said Kathleen. "We're going somewhere quiet, and Thomas is going to sing to me, and not about rabbits either." And away went Margaret and Mike, him singing 'Run Rabbit Run', in between bursts of laughter.

Later, on leaving Kathleen outside the nurses' home, I crossed through an orchard and on to the villa. I was inserting my pass-key in the lock when suddenly the sound of the air-raid sirens began their mournful wailing; the night nurse swiftly rose to his feet as I entered. Instantly, the anti-aircraft guns began to add to the disturbance; and the drone of a flying bomb, directly overhead, cut out, and both of us flew into the linen cupboard where a couple of mattresses were permanently situated on the floor for such situations and we threw ourselves flat, covering our ears with our hands, and none too soon for the explosion followed within seconds of our doing so. We rose to our feet on realising we were not the unlucky target, and went outside the rear entrance. The sky above the village was lit up by red, blue and orange flames; and we expressed the hope that whatever building had been hit, had been empty of humans and animals. Back inside the ward, three or four of the patients were undergoing an unpleasant coughing bout, probably brought on by the shock of the explosion. The night nurse made tea for all of us. I was pleased to observe that the hot drink relieved their coughing. Tea was much better than the usual dope prescription.

The following week I was posted to the villa. I had been advised by some of the staff on my own ward to be wary of a certain orderly: "Don't have anything to do with him," was the general comment.

"What is wrong with him?" I enquired.

"He's a conchie, a yellowbelly," responded one of them.

I soon observed that the staff on the Sanatorium held this conscientious-objector at arm's length. It was only because he had been directed into the work that they grudgingly tolerated his presence. When eventually I got to conversing with this man, who had registered as an 'Objector' on religious grounds, I soon learned that his religious beliefs were as uncertain as my own. On his positive side he was gentle in his dealings with the patients, and that was sufficient for me.

There were no known drugs at the time which could assist in combatting the disease of tuberculosis without endangering the patient further; therefore the sanatorium treatment I supposed, was the only beneficial course that could be undertaken with safety. And of course the villa, built for this purpose, had been ideally situated in isolation so as to gain the most efficient effects of sun, light and uncontaminated air. The worse cases were housed on the veranda, therefore apart from really stormy weather, the veranda windows were kept open twenty-four hours a day, and such patients were confined to it. Only if they recovered sufficiently to advance to the second stage of treatment would they be brought in to the inner ward, and allowed to begin experiencing short spells out of bed; and later, short periods of exercise to build up their resistance to the disease.

Although the patients in the sanatorium received a higher grade of diet than those in the main hospital, one thing they shared in common was the general boredom brought about by the lack of any form of social activity on the wards; the armchair and the unavoidable pastime of space-gazing was their lot.

Though I enjoyed the experience, I was pleased to get back to my own ward.

✳✳✳

One morning on coming out of the ward kitchen I observed Baines, who was in a high state of agitation, pick up a dining chair and begin shattering it on top of the table – while shouting at a nerve-wracking pitch. I stood perfectly still and at once one of the deputy Charges came running out of the office and a couple of nurses rushed in from the dayroom. The four of us closed in on him, and after a struggle got him down on to the floor; his display of exaggerated energy and strength was amazing, yet we managed to undress him, by which time the Charge Nurse had arrived with the straitjacket. The patient's eyes lit up in increased terror as he recognised the medieval restrainer. Despite his by now increased struggles we finally got his arms into the long sleeves then folded them over his chest and secured them into position with the long straps. We soon had him looking like a canvassed corpse about to be buried at sea. Lifting him bodily we carried him into the padded cell and laid him on the floor. After been given an injection, he showed signs of becoming calmer, and though he also seemed drowsy, it was obvious he was doing his utmost to resist the effect of the drug as though he could not afford to relax himself completely and sleep whilst lying there trussed up like a bundle of firewood.

I was aware that the use of mechanical restraint on a patient was permissible under the Lunacy Act, on a medical certificate, but whether the use of the straitjacket was allowed before or after the issue of the certificate I could not tell. Though I could not imagine four staff having to hold down this temporary superhuman dynamo while the Charge phoned the doctor, then awaited his arrival.

However, the few months I had been employed in the hospital, I saw no real possibility of any major disagreement between the doctors or Charge Nurses; they were too much concerned about personal prestige for them to differ on formalities.

Later, the Staff Nurse was preparing Baines for Electro-Convulsive Therapy (ETC); the injection he had been given beforehand was making the patient feel thirsty and no doubt unpleasant, considering his stomach was empty after his fast. Finally the doctor arrived, greeting all of us in his usual business-like manner. After ensuring that all the necessary precautions had been taken and the patient was as comfortable as possible, he set to work. Placing a thin elastic band round the patient's arm he then guided the hypodermic needle into a vein and in about ten seconds the anaesthetic took effect. The Staff Nurse placed a small sandbag in the lumbar region of the patient's spine, then rubbed a contact-lotion on the patient's temple, whilst the doctor directed his attention to the electric machine, with its dials and wires. The whole set-up reminded me of a scene from *Frankenstein*. The headpiece, a perspex horseshoe shape which resembled headphones, was placed in position on the patient's head. The doctor no sooner operated a dial on the machine than the patient went into a convulsion – his limbs jerking violently! What amazed me about the whole procedure was the fact that within a minute of the passing of the electric current, Baines was conscious; though obviously bewildered and apparently unable to assess where he actually was at that moment. It was over in half an hour before he could be encouraged to sit up; the doctor had left by then.

"How are you feeling now, Baines?" enquired the Staff Nurse.

"I've got a headache coming on," he mumbled.

I was not in the least surprised to learn that, considering all the electrical activity sent through his brain. When he was finally coaxed into the dining room, he proved that whatever the shock-treatment had done or not done for him, it certainly had not robbed him of his appetite and he devoured the late breakfast in the fashion of a man just coming off a three days' fast. It was just as well that he was not informed beforehand that he would be having more sessions of the same treatment or that might have dampened his hunger pangs a little.

✷✷✷

One of the most interesting patients on my ward was named Edwards. I had observed him on my first day, sitting at one of the tables in the dining room busy writing notes on large-sized paper, two thick ledgers by his side containing more sheets of his daily journal. He was pensioned-off as far as hospital work was concerned before my arrival, therefore he had all day to work on his reflections; all of his pocket money was spent on writing materials. Before I took to talking to him one of the deputy Charge Nurses had told me about his reputedly amazing background. He was supposed to have been an international con-man, nicknamed the Sugar King! When the First World War came to an end, sugar, among other commodities in Europe, was in short supply. And of course such situations throughout history present a profitable challenge to ingenious and guileful characters like Edwards. Armed with fake bank and merchant references, he obtained a boat, purchased sugar from the producing countries on the strength of his apparent creditworthiness, and sold it on the European markets. Perhaps it had been his aim to make his fortune swiftly then vanish from the scene. But no doubt greed, which often afflicts such clever mortals, had been his undoing, for in time, he was avoiding paying even the harbour dues, which soon led to the International Police getting on his tracks!

He was a temperamental character and often would shun discourse. But on the rare occasions when I found him prepared to be talkative, his tales of past adventures were both revealing and exciting; and whether his yarns were just the products of his imagination, it was not until later when I became first acquainted with the works of Joseph Conrad, that I found his equal in storytelling with a rich nautical flavour. Edwards believed he had been incarcerated in the mental hospital just in order to get him out of circulation.

✳✳✳

When my stint of night duty came around, I was pleased to learn I was assigned to my own ward. At 8.45 p.m., I signed on. When the day shift had left, the Staff Nurse took over the infirmary ward, and I became responsible for the observation of the main sleeping dormitory and side rooms. I lodged myself in the dayroom, at a vantage point which gave me a commanding view of the dormitory, further, I only had to turn my head to the right and if the Staff Nurse required my assistance, he only had to wave his hand. As it was late October, there was a fire in the dayroom, and I built it up until it resembled a blacksmith's forge at full-blast; thinking meanwhile, that decent clothing for the patients might be lacking, along with a supply of baccy and sweets, and the furniture and ward decor might remind one of a prosperous workhouse, but thank heaven there was ample coal, for without it I would have had to resort to the use of blankets and shawls. I uttered a prayer for the safety of the Beavan Boys, and their older comrades working down in the bowels of the earth digging the coal out.

I settled myself comfortably; there wouldn't be much to do during the night apart from the checks in the dormitory and side-rooms every hour, when I would peg the time-points on the dormitory wall, which would indicate to the night superintendent in his office that I was wide awake and doing my rounds. The Staff Nurse signalled to me, and gave me the sleeping draught for Idle. On entering his room I observed he was sitting up in expectation, and he drank the paraldehyde cocktail as though it were a sweet sherry.

"You seem to like that, Idle; you must have a good strong stomach," I commented affably.

"Why don't you go back to Newcastle, you silly bastard?" he replied. "And put that night light out!" he demanded.

"Sorry Idle, the pilot light has to stay on, you know that, you've been here long enough," I responded politely.

"Balls to you, you're like the rest of them in this looney-bin," he said defiantly.

"Goodnight Sir," said I; and surprisingly he allowed me the last word.

After supper I put my feet up and opened a book. The night super had been and gone; he would pay one more visit before the shift was over. I had learned that if by chance he should find a nurse napping it meant trouble for the napper. But to his credit, he was a reasonable and imaginative man, and kept more or less to a regular time routine, and ensured the staff heard him entering the ward. I had also learned that when the chief superintendent was on his nights off, his deputy took over; one of his faults was to vary the times of his rounds, and he also had the habit of creeping up on one silently like an apparition. When he was on duty, everyone concerned gave up all thought of having the odd half hour catnap, at least until after his second and last visit, after that all of the staff were certain he returned to his office, locked himself in and kipped solidly for three hours.

At two o'clock, the Staff Nurse joined me in the dayroom, and on observing that the book I was reading was by Sigmund Freud, he began a discussion on the teachings of that great man, whose theories in the field of clinical psychology had aroused much criticism. My senior colleague proved to be an interesting man to listen to, indeed listening was all I was prepared to do, for I could in no way compete with his years of experience of nursing and studying. However, when he returned to the infirmary, I reflected on all he had said. I could only conclude that as far as Freud's theory of treating the mentally sick by means of psychoanalysis was concerned, that method was not being practised in this colony; if it were, then it must be a failure. Many of the patients in the hospital had been under lock and key for years without any hope of ever living outside the high walls that surrounded the establishment. They were, in my humble opinion, too institutionally dependent to be able to cope on their own. Many of them had never handled money for years, never had the opportunity to shave themselves or to make a pot of tea, let alone prepare and cook a meal or decide when to go to bed, or rise in the morning.

At five o'clock, we began attending to the patients in the infirmary. There were nine patients in the ward at present, seven of whom could be lifted out in turn and on to the commode whilst we stripped their beds and remade them; the other two patients, Martin and Kirkland, were bedfast. After five-thirty, Idle entered the ward and began collecting the urine bottles.

"As soon as you wash the bottles out, Idle, pop into the kitchen. The teapot is waiting for you," remarked the Staff Nurse.

Idle expected this morning perk. He was accustomed to it, no matter who was on duty, but to his credit he always waited until he was told. By the time we had made Martin quite comfortable, Idle was back on the ward collecting up all the soiled linen off the floor; and he was actually humming a tune to himself, a sure indication that he had drained the teapot.

We now began to attend old Kirkland. His bed was situated next to the fireplace, a token that he was well liked by all the staff; he was sixty-eight years old and a nice jovial fellow, with a moon-shaped face. One of his oddities was to hold a two-way conversation with himself at various times during the day, one such interchange of words went like:

In falsetto: "What are you doing in this queer place, dad?"

In bass: "I'm mad, son."

In falsetto: "Who told you you were mad, dad?"

In bass: "The doctor, and the nurses, son."

In falsetto: "Take no notice of the doctor or the nurses, dad, they get paid for telling you that!"

Kirkland never repeated the same two-way repartee in any one day. I was convinced he had been furnished with the material for such performances by one of the deputy Charge Nurses; the Staff Nurse thought not, he believed they were original. If so, they were a credit to his wit.

After completing my tasks in the infirmary, I went and roused the men in the main dormitory, though not many of them were still in the land of nod. Once they were all out of bed and had claimed their own bundle of clothing from the dining table, I went down the corridor to the siderooms where the workers slept, all of whom who were ready dressed, and I released them from the ward to make their way to the main kitchen. I then opened the washroom and pressganged volunteers to assist in washing those patients who for various reasons could not help themselves. Finally, I herded the permanent dayroom patients on to their favourite armchairs; there they would sit and gaze into space until the call for breakfast. By 6.45, I had the ward workers at it in full swing; some making beds, others polishing the floors and cleaning out the toilets, just as the first of the morning shift arrived. It had been a quiet night; of course I realised it wouldn't be so comfortable every night. Grown-up men who were compelled to remain in bed for so long a period were destined at times to become restless.

On leaving the staff dining room I walked slowly through the orchard towards the villa, and bed. Before entering my room, I sought out my batman, and urged him to keep away from the vicinity of my room door with the heavy floor polisher. The majority of the TB patients were suffering from their usual early-morning coughing bout; and the ward's early morning foul air was being added to by the strong smell of the obnoxious floor polish and the aroma of methylated spirits; I was glad to get inside my room and away from it all.

I arose at three o'clock in the afternoon feeling quite refreshed. There were a number of nurses who considered themselves fortunate if they slept three hours a day whilst on night duty; and I wondered how they survived such sleep-starvation.

On arriving on the ward one evening, after the day shift staff had departed, I was about to enter the ward kitchen to have my usual couple of minutes chat with the patient who worked there when I heard him talking to himself, indeed he was having a heated discourse on what he intended doing to Idle the following morning: "You'll what? You'll do what? Take this! And that, you bastard! Have you had enough? No! Then take that, and this." I silently moved the kitchen door sufficiently to observe the kitchen man shadow-boxing, and appearing very pugnacious and determined about it. I had heard from Michael before he went off duty that Idle had upset the kitchen worker at teatime, and had threatened to knock his teeth out. I began whistling to myself, then entered the kitchen, and at once the patient made out he was simply doing his exercises before retiring to his room! The kitchen man and Idle were the only two patients allowed to stay up late; Idle went to bed at nine, the kitchen man at ten o'clock. Idle was the only patient on the ward who didn't care twopence about the exalted position of the kitchen man, and who was reputed to be a handful if he ever cut up rough!

On leaving the kitchen I entered the dormitory. Albert Towel was the only one awake and alert. I sat on the edge of his bed and began talking to him. For many years, on visiting days, Albert had stood sentinel on the corridor near the exit; his visitors had rarely let him down, and often took him out for weekend leaves. Then three years ago, they had suddenly ceased visiting him, but he had continued to hold his post every visiting day, hoping against his fears that perhaps they had died. During our conversation I discovered the reason for his present disquiet and inability to settle down and fall asleep. Another patient, named Plackett, had been taunting him about his weekly vigil beside the ward entrance, telling him that his relatives were dead, and he would be having no more weekend leaves: "You're here, Albert, until you kick the bucket, like the rest of us" he had concluded. I urged Albert to ignore Plackett; and to keep on hoping his visitors would turn up someday. Plackett was the ward nosey-parker, who could always be relied upon to keep the staff informed of any misdemeanour committed by another patient despite never being rewarded for his talebearing.

It was 5.45 by the time we had finished dressing Martin's bedsores; there was Kirkland to attend to yet. Idle came out of the sluice room and commented to no one in particular, "Shall I begin scrubbing the ward?"

"No, of course not, silly man, you can see we haven't finished with Kirkland yet," retorted the Staff Nurse. "Have you made a good job of the sluice?"

"Balls to the sluice," said Idle contemptuously, "I always make a good job of it, I've been doing it long enough."

"All right, bugger off Idle. Go and switch all the lights on in the dormitory and tell them all to get out of bed," said the Staff Nurse. A few minutes later the sound of a fierce commotion reached us from the direction of the dining room.

"That's bloody Idle, I'll bet," remarked the Staff Nurse, and both of us made our way to the scene, to witness Idle and the kitchen man rolling about on the floor locked in each other's arms and grunting like a couple of all-in-wrestlers. The majority of the other patients were continuing to dress, and completely ignoring the two combatants.

"Up, both of you!" called out the Staff Nurse angrily. The kitchen man appeared willing to break, but Idle clung to him as though his life depended on it. Stooping down the Staff Nurse grabbed hold of Idle by his ears and yanked him to his feet.

"Any more of that Idle, and straight into the pad you'll go and you'll stay there."

"Balls to the pad, and you with it," he retorted, freeing himself from the grasp of the Staff Nurse, though not before the latter had landed him a fist in the guts. Idle fell back a step or two, then muttered "Bastard," and swiftly retreated off into the toilets.

At that moment Plackett, the nosey-parker, came cringing forward, that habitual sly grin on his face, "I'll bet the Charge Nurse will be angry when he hears that

Idle has been fighting, sir...!"

The Staff Nurse grabbed hold of him, pulling him close up, "Listen to me Plackett, if you open that big bloody mouth of yours to any of the day staff I'll put you in No. 3 side room when I come on duty tonight, and you will stay there for a week. So bugger off, and begin polishing the dayroom floor."

I knew that Plackett would hold his tongue, his privileges would be at stake otherwise. I was also aware that the Staff Nurse would have every intention of informing the Charge Nurse when he arrived for the seven o'clock shift, so as he would ensure there was no recurrence of the trouble. But both of them would keep it out of their reports; Idle and the kitchen man were two useful workers – they couldn't afford to have either of them confined to bed and so lose their services. I sensed how the Staff Nurse would reason. He knew the kitchen man was out of sight for the rest of the day, and Idle would be too busy scrubbing and polishing to interest himself in past differences; for as a rule he made more use of his sharp tongue than his fists; holding most people in contempt, he preferred his own company.

Ten minutes after his chastising of Idle, the Staff Nurse gave him some tobacco, and patted him fondly on the head. On my way to open the washroom, I heard the patient, Haslam, knocking on his sideroom door; I had overlooked him. On releasing him I bid him good morning, but he ignored me; I considered this to be a good sign, for he usually greeted his morning liberator with a string of sour compliments. But then, I never attempted to irritate him; to laugh and ridicule his known delusions, only made him aggressive, and once in that state, the poor fellow was always the loser.

On coming on duty a few nights later I was not surprised to discover Albert Towel in bed in the infirmary ward; for the two previous days he had refused his food, and wouldn't speak to anyone. I learned that there was nothing physically wrong with Albert apart from his age; it appeared he had decided to relinquish the need to exist and at the end of October, he gave up the ghost. I attended his funeral which took place on a cold sharp morning; also present was the Charge Nurse, his deputy, and of course the hospital chaplain. I was convinced that poor Albert had never once during his long enforced stay in the asylum been shown such respect as was shown that morning at his graveside. Albert Towel had never been able to read or write; a fact which would probably have influenced the officials concerned, who in the beginning, all those years ago, signed the necessary papers to have him detained! I had learned by recent reading that in the days when such as Albert Towel had been certified there had been prison medical officers, and magistrates, who had been convinced that illiteracy denoted mental backwardness. I was of the opinion that the Poor Law System was brought into existence tailor made for the Albert Towels of this world!

✳✳✳

Lately I had begun a correspondence course in chiropody – not that I believed the diploma to be earned would every have any value in my work as a nurse other than learning more about foot abnormalities to the betterment of the patients. But I kept the fact that I was studying chiropody to myself; I didn't wish to provide my colleagues, especially Michael, with an opportunity to pull my leg.

On rising at the usual time in the afternoon, three o'clock, I decided to have a walk around the grounds, in place of going to the staff room and seeking a game of snooker. I would be pleased when my night stint was over. In the far northerly part of the grounds I came across Robert Routledge, a patient, leaning against a fence. This was his favourite location, for apart from the pleasant view he could also observe the trains in the distance, a sight which always seemed to fascinate him. He was sixty years old, and pensioned off. He got his pocket money by rights and so long as he could have a little pipe tobacco he was content. Routledge was one of those inmates who, wisely on his part, had accepted the dull institutional routine from the beginning, giving no trouble, thereby suffering no penalties. Under those circumstances, both staff and patients abided by the philosophy of live and let live.

"Hello Bob. Seen anything interesting on the horizon?" I asked him.

The usual pause, before replying, "There's always something worth seeing, nurse. Trains, horses, birds, cows, airplanes; and the women will be passing this way directly. I have a few words with them, that's if the nurse doesn't mind."

"You won't have had much opportunity to chat up the women in this place Bob," I suggested.

He spat out in apparent disgust. "It's bloody inhuman, I think, nurse. I believe the people who are responsible for the running of these places are bloody mad," said he. "Can you give me a light for my pipe, nurse, please," he asked, bringing out his pipe from his pocket.

Although I didn't smoke myself, I had made it a habit since coming to the hospital to carry a box of matches around with me in order to oblige any patient. He gave a contented sigh after lighting up and taking a deep pull on the stem.

"Well, the war will soon be over, Bob, thank heavens" said I.

"It won't make any difference to me, nurse. I got nothing for fighting in the last one; the dole queue, and the looney bin. I blame the First War for sending me round

32

the bend," he complained.

"Why didn't you seek your discharge when you got better?"

"What's the point, nurse? There was no work outside; no place to go to except the bloody workhouse. Bloody Lloyd George and his government; I would have sacked the lot for kidding the troops about us coming back home to a country fit for heroes."

"How long have you been in here now, Bob?" I enquired.

He directed his gaze back to the distant horizon as though seeking the answer there to my question.

"It must be a long time ago, nurse... My memory is not too good now; it's all that medicine I think, it takes your memory away."

"But you don't get any medicine, Bob," said I.

"Not now, nurse, because I don't need it. But I used to get the medicine; everyone gets dope when they come in here – I would sooner have more baccy and grub!"

On my way back through the hospital corridors towards the staff dining room, I stopped periodically to have a few words with those patients whose parole boundary confined them to the maze of corridors. Their focal points were the many windows which looked out on to the courtyards, gardens, orchards, or driveways; they had to be content with a glimpse of someone moving freely about outside the buildings. If perchance they came across one of the store cats, then that was considered a bonus, for these animals, as though they sensed the limited pleasure and freedom of the corridor wanderers, tolerated the excessive attention directed towards them.

When December arrived I still seemed content in my new abode; I liked the work, and my living conditions were good! Then one morning on rising, and on the spur of the moment, I realised my wanderlust was calling me to move on to fresh pastures. Despite the appeals of Kathleen, Michael and a particular deputy Charge and his wife, and others, I handed in my notice!

My father was probably right: I ought to have been born a gipsy.

Working in the hospital had been for me a unique, even moving experience. I had become convinced that the only symptoms of mental peculiarities visible in a lot of the patients, were of an institutional nature, brought about by an over-powering directive regime, which finally makes the inmate totally dependent on the institution, and its keepers.

Prudhoe Hall

My next job was as a pantryman, then groundsman, at Stowe School, Buckingham (described in my book *At Rest Among The Mighty Dead*). When the school broke-up for the summer holidays, I left, and went to London. I've read somewhere that Stanley had one helluva job in searching for Dr Livingstone in Africa. Well, I reckon his frustrations could not have been any greater than mine, as I searched for accommodation in the bedsitter-land jungle of London in 1945. There were plenty of jobs, but one needs to have a permanent shelter before seeking work. After two whole days of weary footslogging I failed to find a room. I had never realised until then how simple it was to fall by the wayside, and become down-and-out. For two years I lived like a tramp, wandering around the country; looking upon myself as a latter-day Jack London! That period of my life has been described in my autobiography, *Tramp's Chronicle*.

My second nursing experience came about after leaving the road and returning home to Newcastle. I had decided to go to work in a mental defectives' colony, as such institutions were known just before the advent of the National Health Service. I was curious to learn whether the lifestyle for the inmates was any different from that experienced by the patients in the mental hospital.

The long winding main driveway, the spacious grounds, and the administration block, were reminiscent of Bexley, but the similarity ceased there; absent were the prison-like buildings and courtyards, and the endless long corridors. The patients in this colony were housed in large villa-style buildings, though, as I expected, also under lock-and-key; and I supposed, for the majority of them, for no better reason other than the fact they had always been shut in.

On my first morning, I discovered a kind of conveyor belt system of activity in progress. Staff and able-bodied patients worked alongside each other in dressing those who were physically disabled. The first patient I was detailed to dress was a young laddie with cerebral palsy, and as I struggled over my task a perpetual smile graced his almost angelic countenance – which served to create the impression he was enjoying my almost impossible task. When I finally got him dressed I felt such a satisfaction in my accomplishment that I patted him fondly on the head and I too smiled, like a contented cat who had been served with cream. His response was immediate and he gurgled with glee. He was almost inarticulate because of his disability, but he realised all right that I understood everything he was trying to convey to me, and we both felt pleased that we had hit it off together on our very first meeting.

The next chap I attended to had the use of his legs, but not his arms or hands which were so distorted that the normally simple process of putting on a shirt called for great ingenuity on my part. Nonetheless I was convinced that within a week I would be able to dress the most difficult case on the ward in a third of the time it was taking me on my first morning; and without forgetting that I was attending to a human being, and not a bag of sawdust.

When it came to speed combined with gentleness, I was deeply impressed with certain patients who were going about their tasks of assisting the more physically handicapped or more mentally retarded in such a manner that it could be seen that to them their occupation was no act of drudgery, but a labour of love and friendship. I felt that many of these incarcerated Samaritans could teach a lot to their more fortunate brothers, living outside in the world of independence.

No sooner were the assisted inmates dressed, than they were passed over to the next group of workers who washed and dried them and combed their hair. Then other volunteers would transport them from the washroom to the dayroom. The main thing lacking here, as in the mental hospital, was space, which was at a premium. No doubt the planners of such institutions had either intended that smaller numbers would occupy such buildings, or else they had been of the opinion from the beginning that paupers were immune or indifferent to over-crowding and discomfort.

I observed that the devotion of the able-bodied inmates towards their adopted charges continued at mealtimes. Once breakfast had been served, they not only partook of their own meal, but attended to their pals who were sitting next to them at table, or in wheelchairs alongside them: "A spoonful of porridge for you, Albert, then the same for me." After porridge: "A piece of bread and sausage for you, Albert, then the same for me." Then a sup of tea for both! From the moment I had arrived on duty, and on to breakfast time, it was an experience to gladden the heart of anyone who was interested in the sane principles of a co-operative society.

After breakfast I was detailed to supervise two groups of workers: the floor polishers and the toilet-block cleaners. Of the four inmates on the floor, two of them were already on knees and rubbing in the wax polish in a most lavish style whilst the other two, each provided with a heavy manual polisher, stood over them, obviously impatient at what they took to be their slowness in spreading the wax, so eager were they to turn all the available floor space into a kind of skating rink. Having witnessed the same floor polishing method in the mental hospital, I thought it was complete madness with so many patients anything but reliable on their feet. Of course the reason for supervising the ward workers in such institutions is not so much to ensure they do not slacken in their efforts, for most of them are conditioned to make a good job of whatever they are put to; the need to keep tabs on them is because of the danger of some non-worker getting in their way, for most of the workers are so zealous over their task that they would not hesitate to reward any simple patient crossing their path with a hefty swipe.

As soon as the floor polishers were in their stride, I quietly entered the toilet block; the scene I witnessed was what I had expected from my other nursing experience! Such is their effort to make a good job of the toilets, then have the nurse who is supervising them inspect, and hopefully give praise, that the workers do their utmost to place the toilets out of bounds to the rest of the patients until they have completed the task. And so I found that not only were they harassing those patients already using the lavatories, but were attempting to prevent others from entering the block altogether. And the workers didn't take too kindly to my restraining them and allowing the patients access.

"You're a new nurse here. We've been doing this job a long time now," remarked one of them, with vocal support from the other two.

"Now then, listen to me, all of you," I began, "any more backchat and I'll report you to the Charge Nurse; and I'll have you all transferred to Botany Bay; and you'll have to pay your own fare there from out of your pocket-money. Is that what you want?" I asked, wondering whether they could sense the leg-pulling.

The three of them peered at me rather cautiously, maybe pondering whether Botany Bay was some other kind of institution; possibly where awkward patients were sent. After gazing at each other a little bewilderedly they decided not to continue the debate, but get on with their work and attempt to ignore the other patients using the toilets.

I kept glancing into the dayroom to observe how the non-workers were getting along in the process of killing time – those in wheelchairs, or armchairs, and those sprawling on the floor, unable to move. I felt a variety show would go down well in all such institutions; even someone having all of their duty-time to talk to them would be an advantage. But for the numbers on the wards in such places the staff were so few in comparison, and there were so many tasks to do on a morning especially, and so many recurring incidents to keep us fully occupied! Harry, for instance, suffered from fits and had many, and sadly kept landing on his face until he resembled a punch-drunk boxing-booth bruiser. There was Billy, who deliberately banged his head against the wall or any hard surface whenever he felt in the mood and was made to wear a padded helmet for protection, and kept attempting to remove it. There are those who have to be taken to the toilet either because they can't manage on their own, or are too simple to think about going there on their own accord; not forgetting those who are incontinent and at any time may be in need of washing and a change of clothing. And of course in such an institutional environment, there are often a couple of antagonists who may decide to fight each other; completely ignoring the finer points of the Queensbury rules. Someone will begin undressing himself rather prematurely, and so on; the eventualities are countless and continuous.

One afternoon I was playing a game of draughts with a one-armed man; during our second game I asked him how he had lost his limb. He informed me that it was the result of an accident on a threshing-machine whilst out on license and working on a farm. I then enquired of him how much compensation he had received. Not a penny he replied! Later on in the afternoon I took the first opportunity when the Charge Nurse was alone in his office, to mention the case of this patient, merely to have the story verified, and discovered it was true. He then told me about others who had been out on license, and been exploited by certain employers. One man, sent out to work as a kitchen porter in a hotel, was treated as a chattel from the start with poor wages, indifferent food, and long hours. Whenever a licensed patient complained about his conditions, he was always threatened with being returned to the Colony if he didn't hold his tongue and do as he was told. The same tactics of course were used against female patients in whatever employment they were licensed out to, mainly catering, or private service. The irony of all this injustice was that on their return to the institution, such patients may be looked upon as being in breach of the rules that governed their going out on license, and could be penalised.

Coming out of the office, I sat on the floor beside a crippled boy. First I secured his sandals which were coming off with his crawling about the room, then I began chatting to him: How old was he? How long had he been resident in the colony? Did he get visitors? His replies I could not make out, but he appeared to get some satisfaction from talking to me; and that was the point of my exercise! When I was a boy, one of my playmates was a deaf and dumb lad, called Eric. Although I never got round to learning the manual alphabet, I nonetheless became pretty efficient in communicating with him by the means of mime.

I was learning that there seemed to be no time in these mental institutions for such fancies as a real attempt at communication with a patient who was thought of as a hopeless case. However I spent what little time I could talking and miming to these 'silent ones'; and the Charge Nurse, observing my attempts, always encouraged me; and I learned a lot through him, not only because he was a trained psychiatric nurse and his length of service in the colony gave him the added advantage of knowing each patient personally, but also because he did not hold the archaic views held by many of the staff in mental institutions, the 'Them and Us' syndrome. He did not look upon the patients as a race apart, and inferior beings. At bedtime, which was the usual 6.30 p.m., the Charge Nurse always took part in this end-of-the-day routine. With some of them, it was like putting to bed overgrown children: sucking their thumbs and sighing contentedly if any nurse made a fuss of them and tucked them in bed, blessing them and wishing them goodnight. Of course for those patients who were only mildly disabled, being ordered to bed at such an early hour was just another reminder of the unjust classification of 'mental defective' that had been meted out to them from the beginning. The only instruction they received, as far as I could make out, was to keep themselves clean, perform their daily tasks properly and willingly, conform to the rules and not question them – then you'll be all right!

I have always been a great advocate of soap and water – cleanliness to me is second nature, though I must admit I am not a fellow for lounging in the tub for any length of time, just long enough to sing an operatic aria in my mock Italian. But I do have the choice to lie and soak myself if I wish. In an institution where there are from forty to sixty patients on each ward, bathing time, like all other important tasks, is a conveyor-belt affair. There is a set time in which to get every patient bathed then back into the day room; each separate bath marked in the bath book. Bathing usually commenced shortly after breakfast and in this colony the bathing was carried out on the ward in the usual bath tub, and not using showers, as it had been in the mental hospital. Those able to bathe themselves occupied one of the tubs, whilst the other bath was used for those having to be assisted, one nurse doing the washing, another drying the patient, whilst a third attended to the patients' feet. The ward volunteers would be busy dressing the disabled ones; their turn to bathe usually in the afternoon, and sometimes they would be allowed to soak themselves for ten minutes or more, with the observation relaxed!

I had just completed attending to the feet of a particular patient, a most quiet laddie indeed. I had only heard him whisper one request since I had begun work in the colony, when the Charge Nurse spoke to him, "Now then John, I want you to thank the nurse for cutting your toe nails, by singing to him your favourite song."

I didn't expect any response whatever, but surprisingly he began singing:

"In barefoot days when we were just a kid.
In barefoot days these are the things we did.
We would go fishing down by the brook
Using a bent pin for a hook.
We'd fish all day and fish all night.
But the darned old fish refused to bite.
So we'd slide and slide on some old cellar door.
And slide and slide till our pants were worn and tore.
Then we got to go home and get into bed.
Time our mothers got busy with the needle and thread.
Oh boy what joys we had in barefoot days."

What amazed me most was that he could remember the words of the song. I wondered what concealed possibilities there could be lying dormant in the minds of some of these unfortunate people who were never given the opportunity to express themselves. Surely the day must dawn when attempts would be made to find out, but I was convinced such experiments would never come about under the present authoritarian system. This practice of locking up such people into prison-like institutions only increased the suspicions of the public that these unfortunate men and women were dangerous.

One of the rare pleasures for the able-bodied patients, when the weather permitted, was to take them away from the confines of the dayroom armchairs, and out into the woods and fields that surrounded the perimeter of the colony. Any strangers coming up the driveway would be impressed by the chirpy repartee taking place between various patients, for the obvious therapeutic effects were instant; the bottled up tensions would blow away with a March wind. On such walks it was really a benefit that some of the patients were unable to move as quickly as the rest of us for it allowed time for all of them to take in as much of the scenery as it was possible for them to comprehend. And of course the staff were more relaxed and therefore inclined to be jovial and respond to the show of camaraderie from the more able patients.

Once we left the road and entered the woods, the drill could be overlooked and patients allowed to break ranks, to gaze up at the trees where the birds had flown on our approach; some picked wild flowers either for themselves or attempted to press them upon the staff, as a gift. Each patient appeared to have his special nurse and was pleased if the bouquet was accepted; and they displayed jealousy if another patient attempted to beat them to it. Oddly enough certain patients seemed to have adopted a nurse who might have been abrupt towards them. If a rabbit was sighted, the excitement was amazing and no doubt the animals were frightened out of their wits at some of the odd sounds being hurled in their direction. This freedom of movement gained as the result of bringing them out for a walk was certainly an improvement on the limited exercise of the airing courts of the mental hospital. Though for some of the patients, who were of the opinion they ought not to be detained in an institution, having been committed, unjustly in their view, by some Court; or as the result of some dubious IQ exercise, having to be brought out for a walk as if they were children and in need of constant supervision, was an irritation.

Sam, the one-armed patient, moved up to my side; he loved a good natter and was grateful whenever any of the staff engaged him in conversation. I got him talking about his experiences on the farm. Despite his accident and the shabby treatment he had received he still missed the work and would have loved to have spent the rest of his working days on the land.

"What do you miss most of all now that you're unable to work in the farm, Sam?" I asked.

"When I finished work, nurse, and got back to my room which I didn't have to share with anyone else; and I got plenty to eat and I had different clothes to wear after I took off my work clothes. Sometimes, I went in a pub and bought a pint of beer." He laughed gleefully at the thought of having been able to enter a public house like any other free man and order a glass of beer.

"How many pints did you drink then, Sam?" I enquired. He peered at me a little anxiously – as though I was attempting to find him out, even at this late date.

"Only one pint, nurse. I never stayed out late; I always did as I was told." He remained silent for a moment, casting his attention on to the cattle in the nearby field. "I liked watching the cows being milked," he suddenly remarked. "I can milk a cow, you know; I learned that on the farm." He gave out a deep sigh: "I liked having a room to myself; I was saving up to buy a wireless."

"You had a raw deal, Sam; it's an unjust world," I replied.

On my first shift in the colony I found, as I expected, that no one who was able to shave himself was allowed to do so. By this time, bearing in mind my previous experiences, I was coming to the conclusion that the only reason for not allowing able and trustworthy patients to shave themselves was not for any fear they would injure themselves, but simply to continue the long-standing practice of keeping all patients dependent on the Institution. I suppose taking it from the point of view of those whose livelihood was dependent upon such huge establishments continuing to exist, then it would be natural to assume, that if the staff did give up one long-standing rule, it could lead to another and another, and so on until 'Authority' realised they did not require so many staff and doctors. Therefore no one was willing to give up any role that could threaten their future!

There were times when I wondered why trained nurses were necessary in mental hospitals and other colonies; our main tasks appeared to be acting as turnkeys, and keeping mass observation. It stood to reason that very little individual assessment could be made of any inmate under such circumstances and with such numbers under our care. Another problem I thought about was not only whether the patients were institutionalised through their length of stay; but also that many of the long term staff were likewise, at least in a philosophical sense, and that is why they didn't appreciate any need for change!

By the Summer of 1948 I had only been at the colony a few months; but as I was living at home and travelling to work every day, I decided to leave, and went to work in a mental hospital near where I lived; and there I would remain for eighteen months. On leaving the local mental hospital, I once more took to the open road (the story is related in my book *At Rest Among The Mighty Dead*) and remained on it until the close of 1952. For the next two years I settled down at home, and in local employment.

A Home for the Aged

Before 1957, my only acquaintance with the small country town of Biggleswade, in Bedfordshire was having passed through it whilst on the tramp. I now arrived to take up work as a Male Attendant in a home for the aged. The Home had formerly been the local workhouse; and as far as some of the residents were dressed, their clothing could only have been issued from typical workhouse stock. Indeed I later learned that some of the residents were ex-workhouse inmates. I imagined very little had changed for them, apart from the fact they were at liberty to come and go in between mealtimes. The Matron, and her husband who was always addressed by the residents as Master, seemed to be afflicted with a vigorous workhouse mentality.

My duties were in many respects similar to those I had performed while nursing in the mental institutions – attending to the bathing, shaving, hair-cutting, waiting at tables; besides ensuring that the male residents always appeared as presentable as was possible with the poor quality of clothing at hand. As regarding their living accommodation, it was in my opinion totally inadequate. Such a bleak environment may have been considered tolerable, perhaps comfortable, during the Poor Law Workhouse period, but as 'home', to spend one's twilight years in, it was a poor advertisement for the modern National Health Service!

My own accommodation was excellent, though the food and cooking were nowhere near the quality I had been accustomed to in previous institutions. There were two charming young ladies employed at the Home. One, who was single and resident, worked in the sewing room; the other lady, who worked in the laundry, was a divorcee and lived in the town. By the time I arrived on the scene the deputy superintendent was paying attention to the damsel in the sewing room. I naturally cast my attention in the direction of Kathy, the divorcee.

Every afternoon the kitchen was deserted. As I was the only male attendant resident, it was my privilege to retire there for half an hour and make myself a pot of tea. On entering the kitchen one afternoon, I surprised Kathy attending to her suspender – and displaying a most shapely leg in the process: What a lovely figure of a woman, thought I. I offered my assistance, which was refused; so then I asked her for a date. Having been at the Home then for three weeks, I felt sure she must have realised I fancied her.

"I don't go out with strangers," was the reply

"If that's the truth my beautiful flower, how on earth did you ever manage to get married?" I enquired.

She pondered a moment, then smiled. "I'll think about it," she finally replied. "But I can't go out tonight, I've got a whole week's washing to do back home," she added.

"Tell you what, Kate, invite me home, and I'll give you a hand with it; I'm pretty good at the poss-tub, I used to help my mother with the laundry when I was a kid."

She seemed surprised at my offer, and replied earnestly, "You're the first man I've known to volunteer to help a lady with her laundry, or any kind of housework. However I'll let you off this time; and if you wish, I'll go out with you on Friday evening."

Apart from her being a smart good-looking woman, she proved to be a good cook; within a week of our first date I became a regular visitor to her home. Her mother, a widow, who lived two blocks away from Kathy, with her unmarried daughter, took to me from our first meeting!

So the summer rolled by – walks along numerous country lanes, through peaceful woods, and the occasional visit to the village of Sandy, to call on her Aunt, who was confined to bed as an invalid. From the village we would stroll up into Sandy hills, where I discovered the acoustics were perfect for serenading my love. Everything was so tranquil; a ready-made home, and a pretty colleen willing to become mine for keeps. I was not being pressurised to come to any swift decision, apart from a gentle hint from her mother that Kathy would make me a good wife. I realised that a struggle was beginning to take place within me – between common sense on the one hand, and the urge to move on, on the other. Common sense lost!

Unknown to Kathy, I began scanning the vacancy columns of the nursing journals, and also that of *The Times*. After a while I was successful in obtaining a post as a male attendant, in a reception centre for the homeless, situated in St Albans. On handing my notice in, I begged that they did not pass the word around, however, someone, probably in the office, informed Kathy. She immediately handed her own notice in, despite my pleas that if she would withdraw it I would send for her once I had settled down – nothing doing. My warning that I was an incurable drifter was in vain; she knew I was heading for St Albans, and was determined to accompany me!

The Spike

Needless to say, when I had applied for the post as Reception Centre Attendant, I never let on that I had myself been on the road, and a user of the Spike; to do so would have been as foolish as an applicant for the position of a Prison Officer admitting he was an ex-prisoner!

My post was a residential one, so when we arrived in St Albans, Kathy had to put-up in a hotel. Within days she had secured a resident nursing post in one of the mental hospitals in the area.

My first week's duty was on the late shift, 2p.m. until ten; under the personal surveillance of the Senior Officer. At six o' clock I opened up the gate to allow the awaiting wayfarers to enter. I sat at the desk, facing the small wicket window, interviewing the vagrants who were seeking a night's shelter; my Superior stood in the background monitoring my progress. It was on the fourth evening, just after eight o'clock, when a particular wayfarer appeared on the scene. My heart sank, I was looking at a former brother tramp whom I had once worked alongside for a whole week in some hotel kitchen, washing pots and pans and scrubbing floors. I winked at him, and surely my countenance at that moment ought to have convinced even a fool that I was bidding him not to let on that he knew me; but in vain.

"Hello there!" he called out in complete surprise. "Fancy meeting you here…"

I interjected abruptly, "I don't know who you think you're talking to my friend…"

He in turn was about to butt in, apparently to attempt to refresh my supposed lapse of memory, when the Senior Officer stepped forward and addressed me, "Do you know this man Mr Callaghan?"

"Never met him before, Sir," I lied regretfully.

"Now then," said the supervisor to the vagrant, "don't come the old dodge in this place, mister. Speak only when you're addressed, otherwise take a walk."

I then took down the particulars from him, comparing them with the details on his record card, he being a regular visitor, got him to sign the register, then sent him over to the scullery to receive his supper from the hands of the Tramp-Major! I felt rotten with myself, but there had been no other way out; to have acknowledged being on familiar terms with a man whose vagrancy record confirmed he had been on the road for many years would have been equal to admitting having myself once been a tramp, and I would have faced ignominious dismissal.

A few weeks later, two more old road acquaintances, Irish tinkers, husband and wife, entered the centre; but thankfully by now I worked alone on duty. In the privacy of the vagrants' bathroom I was able to have a quiet talk with him and give him a few shillings. "Give my kind regards to the wife," said I, as I led him to the sleeping dormitory. I had first met these two travellers in 1946, in the Lake District, and again the following year, sheltering inside the tomb of some aristocratic lady, during a severe snow storm. Here they were, many years later, still on the road. Like many other vagrants I had known, they wanted nothing doing with permanent employers, landlords and officialdom. The occasional visit to the workhouse for a night's kip they looked upon as unavoidable.

My job in the Reception Centre was to some degree similar in nature to my work in the mental institutions – ensuring that those under my care were fed, bathed, sent to bed, told to rise; and put to work the next morning. While the vagrants were in there, they were as much incarcerated as the patient in the mental hospital or the man inside prison; they were subjected to strict rules and discipline. What manual work needed doing in the Centre, once the vagrants had been released at noon, was performed by certain individuals who had been given the opportunity to rest-up for a while; and who were thus known by their fellow wayfarers as Tramps-Major. A number of these men, providing they were of employable age, were sometimes offered the opportunity of rehabilitation, being introduced to prospective employers, usually as kitchen porters in transport cafés or hotels. Hard unglamorous work, split-shifts, poor accommodation, poor food, low wages, and scant rest-periods. As a result, the majority of the men who accepted the offer remained in the post just long enough to save up a few pounds then packed it in. On doing so of course they would bear in mind that there was one particular Spike they would have to give the go-by in the future, on their endless journeys searching for the rainbow's end!

The most distressing sights I witnessed inside the reception centre, apart from the obvious plight of the old men and women dossers, who were totally unwanted in the world, and totally inadequate to face the life of homelessness were the young families who had been evicted by some unscrupulous landlord, and directed to the Reception Centre by the authorities as a temporary measure. There was no separate accommodation for such emergencies; the centre was only intended as a night shelter for the housing of tramps; therefore the wife would have to sleep in the dormitory alongside the female vagrants, and the husband slept in the same dormitory as the male tramps, or perhaps in one of the cubicles where the Tramps-Major usually slept. If the couple had a young baby, then the welfare officer had to be called in. On two occasions I observed verbal sparks flying between young mothers and the welfare officers, the latter insisting that on account of the baby both mother and infant would have to be transferred to separate accommodation, at another address, thus leaving the husbands behind as unwilling lodgers in the Spike. It does not require much imagination for any young wife faced with such a situation to work out that if she is separated from her husband under such conditions, he could become dispirited with the arrangements and decide to vanish. She would be already sufficiently incensed at the action of her landlord at putting them on the street, and placing them in a position liable to split up the family without officialdom, through its various offices, unwittingly assisting in the process!

Though there were no female staff employed in the Centre, there was a home for the aged next door, in the same grounds; so every time we signed in a female vagrant, we would phone the home, and a female nurse would come in and supervise the bathing of the woman and examine her clothing for any signs of lice.

Christmas Day in the Workhouse! At such a time of the year it was usually the old and the infirm who voluntarily entered the gate, for they were given the otherwise rare opportunity of remaining in the Centre for three clear nights, which would cover Christmas Day and Boxing Day. It could be taken for granted that any young vagrant who sought asylum in the Spike on Christmas Eve, only did so because he hadn't the means to celebrate the festive season in the company of jovial Bacchus! However, for two whole days the normal strict discipline was relaxed, and the overdone routine of scrubbing tasks was suspended. Three meals a day were supplied from the kitchen of the Home; and this was supplemented by an abundance of cakes and sandwiches sent in from outside by certain benevolent bodies, who usually respond in such fashion during the annual festive season. And the staff were less authoritative, even wishing the vagrants a Happy Christmas, though I knew from personal past experience that all this once-a-year bonhomie didn't fool the wayfarers. They knew that once Boxing Day was over, the seasonal Christian sentiment being displayed by all concerned about their welfare would be put away for another year. No alcohol was permitted but a few cigarettes were distributed. For two whole days the men sat in the dining room, eating, drinking tea, smoking, reading old newspapers and magazines, gossiping, and planning their next move for when they left the Centre. Such a dull festive season could have been experienced in any workhouse at any time in the past! Scrooge, before his sudden reformation, would have applauded the austerity applied to such homeless shiftless characters.

Practising Chiropody

Spring Time, 1959. Not only was Kathy fed up with her work in the mental hospital, but with our separate living accommodation; she was determined to act. She scanned the vacancy columns of *The Times* and in a short space of time she found a double position which entailed managing a small bed and breakfast hotel in London; and rather reluctantly I accepted the move. But this didn't last long; both of us found the work too tying, indeed it was a twenty-four-hour job, and with low wages. Within a month we were installed as managers over a luxury block of flats, in Earls Court! On being offered the post, it was impressed upon me by the dapper-looking millionaire proprietor that the House was a respectable one; and it was up to me, to see it remained so!

By the end of our second week in the post, I had mentally catalogued every tenant in the house, from the basement to the top of the building – all six floors. I came to the conclusion that the whisky-drinking would-be-novelist was not the only quaint character residing in the house, and those who were legitimately employed, were few indeed. There were at least four or five call girls, a lesbian prostitute, a dubious looking so-called doctor whose only visitors were more dubious-looking women, and a number of students whose only study appeared to be the female form. A few weeks after taking over, I had to eject the lesbian tenant for keeping a rough-house; her language was the most poetic I'd heard from any woman; her use of foul words was astounding.

However come Autumn, we were still holding the fort. Then early one morning, my own door bell began ringing with insistence. Going downstairs and opening the front door, four plain-clothes policemen displayed their warrant cards in my face! I had to accompany them down into the basement and was ordered to open up the room door of one of the resident call-girls, where they arrested a man, who at that moment of our entry had jumped out of bed. Before the posse had left, the officer-in-charge said to me, "I wouldn't remain in a job like this! Think about it!"

We left the respectable house within five days. Back to St Albans we went. I took up work again in a mental hospital; Kathy went to work in a branch of Woolworths.

One evening in January 1960, I happened to read in a medical journal, of the shortage of chiropodists. I began thinking of all the practical experience I'd had in the hospitals; and I possessed a Chiropody Diploma. It was only a correspondence document, but my knowledge of the profession was real and practical. I told Kathy we were going north, to Newcastle, my home town, to begin a chiropody practice. I realised I wouldn't be able to afford the rent for suitable premises in St Albans. Kathy was as enthusiastic as myself.

In Newcastle we found a nice furnished flat, in the large house of a retired business woman – a JP. She was a grand old lady who loved a joke, and a noggin. After a search for vacant premises to let, I finally took over an empty shop in Stanhope Street, in the west-end of the City. I don't think the shop had been blessed with soap and water, and paint, internally or externally for at least two decades, during which time it had been used as a plumber's store room. It mattered not. Such was our eagerness to become established that we scraped twenty years of grime and grease off the floors and walls, then painted inside and outside. The following week when the landlord called to collect his rent he almost walked by the premises such was the transformation. Then came the fittings, furniture, lamps, etc; in truth after purchasing a supply of dressings and other materials and having business cards printed, we were broke. So Kathy volunteered to find work until I began to earn. However, for someone who was becoming accustomed to living in a fool's paradise, I was extremely happy, and confident!

One thing I learned very early was that the women who came to have their feet attended to were rather disdainful of any advice on the question of suitable footwear; these dear ladies, of whatever age, were seeking remedial miracles, not my preaching about what type of footwear they ought to adopt. One thing I was not learning was to treat every individual client in a cool detached professional manner, and not be guessing, at the completion of their treatment, whether they could afford to pay my fee in full, if at all! Anyone who appeared down on their luck I could not, for the life of me, charge the full fee. Therefore I made it my custom to charge only the cost of any dressing or foot aids I provided. Consequently, it soon became apparent to me that these unfortunate people were informing their relations, friends and neighbours all about my painstaking and cheap treatment. Had I come into a fortune just then, I would gladly have opened my doors to these needy folks and treated them all free of charge. However, the fact was not only that I was not making a small profit, I was not even earning any wages, only sufficient to pay rent and purchase dressings. Sadly I came to the conclusion that I must close up shop.

My aim now was to get back into nursing in the mental hospitals. Selling off the effects of the business, I shared the proceeds between us. By now Kathy was scanning the vacancy columns of *The Times*, for a double position in domestic service. That decided my next move. At the first opportune moment I was out of the lodgings, and on my way to London on my own.

In the capital I commenced the weary old trail of searching for a furnished room. In the evening I gave up the hunt, and entered the Euston Station buffet for a drink. On coming out of there, my eyes happened to light on a poster advertising the merits of the Dublin Boat Train. After a few minutes' mental debate, I purchased a return ticket to Dublin, thinking that if I didn't make a success of chiropody in Dublin within a month, I would come back to London and forget my dream of becoming self-employed.

It was a lovely night when the boat sailed away from Holyhead towards Dun Laoghaire. Below deck in the saloon bar I struck up a conversation with an Irish building worker, returning home to Dublin on holiday.

"What's your work, Pat?" he enquired, after informing me what his own occupation was.

"I'm a chiropodist," I replied.

"A foot doctor!" said he, looking mighty impressed. "My God, I'm pleased to have met up with you."

"I'm not a doctor," said I, not wishing to create a false impression, especially when a number of other passengers around us were interesting themselves with our conversation.

"Away with you man," began he, "you're too modest. You will never get anywhere in this bloody world unless you impress people you hold a good opinion of yourself. You're a medical man, and there's no two ways about it."

He insisted on buying me a drink. After we had downed our third pint together, he implored me to look at his feet. Though by now quite a number of saloon passengers were off to sleep, we still had about seven of them gathered around as I opened my grip, donned my white coat, laid out my instruments, and then got to work on his angry-looking corns.

"What steady hands he has," remarked a young colleen, sitting near at hand.

"And him drunk too," replied her friend.

I decided not to refute the slander, as I felt sure it was meant as a compliment.

On arriving in Dublin, I bade farewell to my fellow passenger. After a good breakfast, I began room hunting. Walking up O'Connell Street, I entered Parnell Street. Going into a corner shop to purchase a bar of chocolate, I decided to enquire where I might find a furnished room. The shopkeeper, a middle-aged inquisitive

looking woman, studied me a few moments. Finally, appearing satisfied, she directed me to a Mrs —, living in North Great George Street, which led off Parnell Street:

"Tell her I sent you then it shall be all right; she knows I'm a good judge of character. You'll be all right there, she's a good woman. Tell her I sent you, don't forget, mention me. And anything you ever want, you can get it here, I'm open all
day."

On presenting myself to the lady I had been sent to I was shown a large front
room on the first floor. On replying to her query as to what work I followed, she
began smiling broadly, to my discomfort.

"Tell me again, what work you do, sir!" she appealed to me.

"I'm a Surgical Chiropodist, madam," I replied, beginning to feel foolish, for by
now she was chuckling merrily away to herself.

"Is that right now. An' what kind of work is that? What do you do exactly?" she
asked, appearing determined to get to the bottom of the mystery.

"I attend to people's feet complaints," said I simply.

"Oh, I see now. You cut out corns. I'll wager you'll be run off your own two feet,
for you'll be that busy in Dublin. You've come to the right place. You'll make your
fortune; you'll soon need a car to get you around."

That's what you think, Missis, thought I, for I intended operating my business
from my room. And so the very next day I walked around the area placing detailed
postcards advertising my services in various corner shop windows!

A week later, I began to form the opinion that everyone in Dublin must have perfect feet, either that, or whoever was glancing at my cards, was looking upon them
as the work of a practical joker. However, I assured myself there was time yet! On
exploring Dublin in the evenings, I found the working-class areas very similar to
those of my boyhood neighbourhood, in the respect that the corner shops appeared
never to close their doors, and one could purchase almost anything up to midnight.
And at such late hours I would come across the odd kid, selling newspapers, outside the hotels on O'Connell Street. Every time I encountered one of those wide-
awake lads, I felt as though Old Father Time had turned the clock back a few years,
and that I was looking at myself on the main terrace of my home town.

On my first Sunday evening, I went out in time for the pubs' opening at seven
o'clock. To my amazement – and dismay – I discovered the public houses were
closing their doors, having been open since midday. But I soon learned that some
of the pub windows were heavily curtained, or blacked-out, solely to cope with this
Sunday restriction! I observed a man tap on the window of one particular public
house, the door opened and he swiftly slipped inside. Allowing a moment to pass,

I gave the signal also, and was admitted. Thereafter on a Sunday evening getting a drink was no problem. Of course I could have frequented the large hotels, no problem there; but I was after being in the company of real people.

During my second week I attended to three women, and one man. Yet again, I hadn't the heart to charge a full fee; they appeared to be worse off than myself. Then what could I expect by having to advertise my services through the medium of corner shops; it ought to have been obvious to me that I stood to get the poorer client seeking my aid, for no well-shod person seeks the service of a chiropodist in working-class quarters. After the third week I realised I could not afford to continue paying rent, and cater for a healthy appetite and a keen thirst on a non-existent income. I decided I would have to return to London and seek a wage-earning occupation, and forget my dream of becoming self-employed as a professional worker!

Then on the Monday morning of my fourth week, I suddenly got the urge to go tramping for a few days. First I sold off some of my surgical instruments, and personal gear and purchased a haversack, a waterbottle, and a thick army blanket. After a little discussion with the railway station master, he agreed to allow me to lodge my suitcase for a week or so, whilst I went on the ramble around the countryside. My landlady was sorry I was leaving, but was understanding of my financial problems. With my waterbottle filled, and a supply of bread and cheese and an onion in my haversack, I set off.

My first stop was at Dun Laoghaire; I sat down overlooking the pier and attended to my appetite, pondering meanwhile where to head for. Glendalough! Why not visit the shrine of St Kevin now that I had the opportunity? When I arrived at Dalkey, I debated with myself as to whether I ought to go out of my way and pay a visit to the one-time home of Bernard Shaw. After a little hesitation, I decided to explore the town of Dalkey instead; I felt sure the ghost of the Irish Bard would understand. The town was worth seeing; the Town Hall, which was a restored old castle, was not the only Civic Centre I had come across on my travels which had been created from the ruins of some historical monument – wonderful romantic sights I find them. Purchasing more rations, I set off towards Enniskerry.

My long experience as a wayfarer taught me that the tramp is treated with a certain reservation, and sometimes deep suspicion, in the English countryside; but here in Ireland, I was surprised at the keen curiosity shown towards me on the road, not only by the average countryside native, but by the native motorist, and visitors. "Good day to you. Where you heading for? Where have you come from?" were some of the usual remarks and enquiries directed at me in a friendly manner.

Enniskerry was my first camp, and I treated myself to three pints of beer before searching out a secluded kip, and reading a few poems until failing light called a halt. Minutes later I was off into the land of nod, hoping, if I were to be disturbed during the night, that my visitors would be leprechauns, promising to lead me to a crock of gold.

The following morning, I had walked no more than a couple of miles when I was offered a lift by a motorist; I hadn't been seeking a lift, indeed I was enjoying the landscape too much to bother myself over thumbing one; however I accepted, considering the kindness of the gentleman who was offering it! I had formed the opinion during my years on the tramp, that most drivers, especially those in private motor cars, offer men of the road a lift because they are curious about such wayfarers, and why they lead such a shiftless and lonely existence. A few of such drivers entertain romantic views of the man of the road, and this is soon revealed by their mode of quizzing! The gent who had offered me the lift, proved to be one such individual, and his romantic notion that I was a kind of King of the Highways and Byways, seeking, and no doubt finding, adventures on my travels, which the dull average citizen never dreams of, was greatly enhanced on learning that I was on a pilgrimage to the Shrine of St Kevin. This I had related deliberately in such a poetic fashion as to fire his romantic ideals of me. I thought such kindness as his deserved to be rewarded in the only way possible. He even went out of his way and took me right up to the valley of Glendalough.

Even if the driver had not pointed out the entrance of the Cathedral ruins, I would have known when I observed the majestic old arches. A young priest I had talked to in Dun Laoghaire had described the scene to me. Before leaving me, my benefactor pressed upon me a ten-shilling note: "Say a prayer for me whilst you're there," said he, before driving off.

Being fascinated with all historical monuments, whether they be castle, priories, churches, even ancient cemeteries, I was reluctant to leave the scene, and so decided to sleep in the vicinity; and keep company with the ghost of St Kevin. As I sat looking up towards the area which I took to be the location of the cave where 'Kevin' was supposed to have lived in as a hermit, I pondered on the legend relating to one aspect of his life: his love for Kathleen; and how he was supposed to have thrown her out of his cave down to her death after his vision or delusion that he was chosen to lead the religious life. If the legend had any truth in it, I wondered why he had been placed on the list of Saints after such a cruel act of betrayal! But then again, I had read of other individuals who had been added to the Roll of Saints, despite a dubious track-record on earth.

Next morning I continued my roaming and for a few more days I thoroughly enjoyed the experience of the tramping life, being continuously surrounded with a panoramic paradise. Further, there were those rare human encounters, other wayfarers who greeted me instantly as a travelling friend, someone to chat openly with without reserve; with a keenness to explore each other's mind, unconscious of being nosey-parkers.

Then back to Dublin. Two days later I arrived in London with about five pounds. I invested half the amount on a supply of Old Moore's Almanacks, and went round door to door, selling them; at night I slept in common lodging houses.

Babyminder in a Nightclub

Having always been keen on debate, and Kathy being aware of this. I was not at all surprised when she discovered me at Speaker's Corner, Hyde Park. She was by then employed as a housekeeper for some titled Lady, residing in Westminster. She had informed her employer from the start that she was married, and that I was working away for a short period. Kathy had been convinced she would eventually find me. So, happily, I was able to move out of the doss-house, and into a well furnished basement flat. In the meantime, I continued going out every morning at the same time, to a new job, as far as Kathy's employer was concerned; in reality I went on canvassing with my Almanacks. But such working arrangements were not to Kathy's liking, she would have preferred to have me employed under her close scrutiny; I had vanished once, and she didn't wish to risk it again. So, back to searching the columns of *The Times*, for a double post! Within two weeks of our reunion, she had found us a resident post in a nightclub, down near Ascot racecourse.

The club, which had formerly been a large private residence, stood in its own grounds, which were sadly neglected, and naturally I thought my main occupation would be to restore the grounds to their former glory, signs of which could still be traced. So I never imagined that apart from trimming the privet, and sawing logs for the stove, my main occupation would be baby-minding, while Kathy got on with the cooking and washing.

The proprietors, in their late thirties, had two children, a boy aged eleven, and a baby girl. The baby, like all toddlers, was a lovely little creature; the boy possessed the most unhappy, yet the most mischievous looking face that was possible to imagine in a boy so young. From the moment we were introduced to him, I sensed he was attempting to weigh us up; on me especially, he bestowed a particular elfin-like scrutiny, which undoubtedly was meant to inform me: any nonsense out of you Mister, and you'll regret it. After a meal, Kathy and I went upstairs to unpack. At eight o'clock, she went downstairs and returned with the baby; the parents would now have to begin attending to the business of the club. I nursed the baby so that Kathy could watch a favourite programme of hers on the television. A few minutes

later, the boy entered; he glanced at the screen, and obviously the current programme met with his disapproval for he briskly moved forward to the set, and
switched channels, then sat down on the carpet to view his choice.

"What on earth are you playing at," retorted Kathy; "I was watching the other
side – can't you look at your mother's television downstairs?"

"She's watching the same as you," said he, "so I'm going to watch what I want
on this one."

I said to Kathy, "Switch it back to your own channel; never mind young
Herbert."

He looked up at me, a scowl upon his countenance, "This is not your house! I'll
tell my mother if you don't let me watch what I want!" He rose to his feet and
attempted to stop Kathy approaching the set. I handed over the baby to her; then led
the boy to the door:

"Go downstairs, son, and argue with your dad if you wish" said I.

"He's not my dad," he called out angrily, "he's my stepdad."

"Whoever he is, son, go and tell him I don't want you barging in here and taking over." Instead of going downstairs, he went into his bedroom and banged the
door after him.

Next morning I rose early and lit the kitchen stove, and prepared breakfast for
Herbert, Kathy and myself; whilst she attended to the baby. The boy arrived in the
kitchen first. I set before him sausages, scrambled eggs, tomatoes and toast.

"Who cooked the breakfast?" he asked, due no doubt to the absence of Kathy,
who was upstairs with the baby.

"I did. Is there anything wrong with it?" I enquired tactfully.

"No! It looks good to me. I didn't know men could cook; my stepdad can't
cook," he remarked critically.

After completing my own meal, I went out into the bar to clean up and wash the
glasses. A few minutes later Herbert looked in, and asked if he could have a bottle
of pop for school. I gave it to him.

"You won't tell my stepdad that you gave me this?"

"I don't tell tales, Herbert. Just be a good lad, and you and I will get along fine."

As he was going out, he turned and asked, "Will you play at cowboys, with me
sometimes? I've got two gunbelts and two guns."

"Cowboys!" I uttered in surprise. It had been some years since I had ridden my
make-believe horse on that imaginary range. Well, why not, thought I; he was obviously a lonely kid. "You want me to play at cowboys? All right, I'll play with you
when you return from school," said I; and even looked forward to it.

"My mother and my stepdad will be out of bed then; we better wait until Saturday," said he sounding regretful.

"That won't make any difference to us, we'll play down at the bottom of the garden; perhaps your stepdad will play with us," I remarked with a smile.

"My stepdad only plays cards," he replied scornfully.

On finishing my work in the bar, I went to the woodshed and sawed sufficient logs to serve the rest of the day. After a cup of tea, Kathy placed the baby into its pram, and I went out with it, as proud as any dad with his first ever experience.

After teatime, I told Kathy I was going out into the garden to play cowboys with Herbert. She let me know what she thought of my mentality before going upstairs with the baby! We were shooting it out in genuine Hollywood style behind the trees, when I suddenly observed Herbert's stepfather peering critically at me, from behind a bush near the driveway. On realising I had spotted him, he rewarded me with a dismal look before returning to the house! There goes another poor creature starved of a sense of humour, thought I. As far as I was concerned I was thoroughly enjoying the exercise; playing at cowboys when I was a lad was my main pastime.

One morning whilst out shopping, I called into a café for a cup of tea. I had no sooner sat down, than an elderly woman aged about sixty, and dressed in the style of the 1930s, entered, ordered a tea, looked around her, and appeared to single me out. Sitting close up to me, she first made a brief study of my countenance, and seeming satisfied with the results, she sipped some tea, then began addressing me, in a quiet confiding manner.

"Listen to me, young man! The *Queen Mary* has just sailed from New York, this morning; on board are two Russian spies. They're sending out messages on their radio, to my Doctor in the local hospital; he's not a real doctor, you understand, he's only disguised as a doctor, and wears a white coat; and he hates cats. The Russians want this doctor to go to my address and kidnap the man who lives in the flat above my own; because he's in arrears with his rent. And this man, who lives upstairs, keeps hammering at my ceiling; I think he's attempting to break-in and steal my money in order to pay his rent. So when you leave here, young man, phone Scotland Yard, and tell them to meet the *Queen Mary*, when she docks at Southampton, and take the radio off these Russian spies, for they are always tuning in to my mind!"

And so she rambled on. I pondered on how such individuals could sound so articulate with their delusions. I felt sorry for the poor woman, and wondered whether her doctor was aware of her mental condition. Though if he was, I realised he was probably prescribing the usual suppression drugs that were served out in the mental hospitals, and which cured no one! I thought it was a great pity that the

National Health Service, did not allow, and even encourage, imaginative doctors to prescribe fresh food, fruit and vegetables, and supplementary vitamins if necessary, to such mentally disturbed individuals. The cost of providing such people with a healthy diet could be offset at the expense of the huge profits made by the various drug-houses.

In time, young Herbert was trailing after me on an evening, and addressing me like an elder brother. Gone was his apparent rudeness and defensiveness, most of the time. One Saturday afternoon, he volunteered to assist me in sawing logs.

Suddenly with concern in his voice, he remarked, "You won't leave here, will you?"

I rested the saw, and peered at him, before replying cautiously, "Well, I haven't thought about leaving. But what made you ask that question Herbert?"

"'Cause everyone else has left, after a little while," said he.

"Did you get on well with them?" I inquired.

"Sometimes I did. But none of them played at cowboys with me, you're the only one."

"Have you no pals of your own age, Herbert?" I asked tactfully.

"Only at school," he replied. "Are you staying here for good?" he asked, seeking reassurance.

I knew I could not commit myself to this, and remain honest with the lad. "I can't answer that question, son, I wish I could. No one can answer questions like that, because no one knows what tomorrow may bring!"

I pondered on why two people with two young children to care for, took over a large house and utilised part of the ground floor as an all-night drinking and gambling club. I supposed the profits were tempting enough to make up for living such an unnatural existence; up all night, and sleeping well into the following afternoon; with only Sunday night free. Even then, they couldn't go out together, for on that evening Kathy and I had our time off. Whatever money they were making out of the venture, the kids were the losers. They had to rely upon caretaker parents; and due to the very limited free time, and long working hours, no child-minders remained long at the post. Young Herbert was only too well aware of this.

The year was drawing to a close when Kathy and I left. Our only regrets were on leaving the children, whom we had come to love. At Kathy's suggestion, we travelled to Bedford. Within hours of arriving there, we were comfortably lodged in the house of an Italian family.

The Private Asylum

Our accommodation, which was really an independent flat at the top of the house, was excellent, and the rent reasonable when compared to the rents in London. On Christmas Day, the family invited Kathy and me to spend it with them! No television on that day, Christmas was spent in the fashion they were accustomed to back home in Italy: music, wine and song. I never sang so much in one day in all my life. How much wine we all drank I can't tell; what I am certain of, and this applied all round, that the continuous singing of operatic arias appears to prevent one from succumbing to the effects of too much booze. None of us got to bed before four o'clock in the morning, yet all of us were up six hours later singing *La Donna-e-Mobile*, as we prepared breakfast; no visible signs of a hangover on anyone in the house, even the cat was in find fettle after its late night Martini mixed with milk!

I soon discovered that the singing of arias from various operas was not a pastime of theirs solely reserved for Christmas; when this family were all together, they sounded like some operatic society rehearsing for an approaching production. And with them being ever so friendly, I always joined in whenever I was in the house. Not knowing the words to any of these arias, I sang in my own, bathroom Italian style, having had ample practice at it during my busking days on the road, and which sounded pretty effective, though I must add it created much hilarity among my Italian hosts. Indeed, I got so carried away with this domestic soap opera atmosphere, that for a few days at least I refused to converse with Kathy, except in an operatic fashion, even if I was requesting for a button to be sewn on to my shirt, but in time she refused to respond to such nonsense, as she termed it.

The following month, January 1961, I found employment as a male nurse in a private mental hospital, run by a doctor whose own residence was situated in the grounds.

When I entered the ward on my first morning at 6.55 a.m., and secured the door behind me, I observed a small thin man, standing in the corridor fully-dressed and holding a small attaché case. He peered at me most expectantly, then enquired in a soft spoken voice:

"Have you come to take me home, sir?"

"You haven't had your breakfast yet," I replied, leaving him to continue his lonely vigilance.

One of the sideroom doors opened on the same corridor and another patient appeared; he scrutinised me rather dubiously, before enquiring, "Are you a doctor, or a nurse, which?"

I smiled at him, "I'm a nurse. And good morning to you," I replied. "I hope you have had a good night."

"Never mind good morning, or whether I've slept well or not," said he irritably. "Shall I set the tables for breakfast?"

"You may as well, if that's your regular job," I replied.

In the dayroom I was introduced to the dayshift nurses, and also to the night nurses who were preparing to depart. My first surprise in this asylum was to discover that male and female nurses worked alongside each other on male wards. I had never experienced this in other mental hospitals, though I for one was fully in favour of the principle. Of course segregation was practiced as far as the patients were concerned.

After donning my white coat I was put to making beds; I observed that apart from the patient who was assistant-voluntary in the dining room laying the tables, no other patients took a hand in any of the daily chores. Then again I had not expected it; these patients were Wards of Chancery, not pauper patients; they pleased themselves whether they mucked in or not. There could be no work persuasion in this institution, nor would there be any incentive to bribe with the paltry means of sweets or cigarettes, as these patients would be well provided for in pocket money.

Breakfast consisted of porridge, then bacon and french fries, bread and butter and tea. During the meal I kept to my usual observation routine, ensuring that there were no human ostriches present, who might suddenly decide to swallow any item of cutlery. After the meal came the distribution of the suppression pills to assist in keeping ward tranquillity. The staff breakfast was identical to what the patients had enjoyed. I was soon to learn that the patients and staff usually shared the same diet, and good food at that. Our employer certainly did not stint on grub. Of course, good food, and good wages, and the Director paying a higher salary than the public bodies did, meant that the staff had more than supervisory duties to perform. Chores, which in a public mental hospital would have been carried out by the patients, had to be done by us, the staff, and why not?

I got busy with the floor polish and bumper, making the dormitory, corridors and dayroom floors shine up like mirrors, which is the state usually preferred in most such institutions, despite the inherent dangers of walking upon them. After the coffee break, I was about to begin dusting, another over-done occupation in such places, when the Director came on the ward, and invited me and another male nurse to accompany him outside. He led the way to the woodshed, and without ceremony, suggested we spend a couple of hours sawing logs for the numerous open fires in the building. We were delighted at the prospect.

In the afternoon, both of us were detailed to take a number of patients around the grounds for exercise. The estate was small in comparison to the spacious grounds of the public hospitals I was accustomed to, nonetheless the small woods and pleasant gardens were sufficiently large for the size of the hospital and the number of patients it contained. On coming across a group of female patients with their escorts, we stood a few minutes in order to allow a little human get-together between both parties. A little handshake, and perhaps a stolen kiss is a tonic for all concerned; even love notes and small gifts passed and received, were all permissible in this small colony of eccentrics; then for the present we all bid each other goodbye. On the fringe of the woods we came to a deserted sculptor's studio; on enquiring of my colleague, about this, I learned that the workshop had once been used by the Doctor's daughter, who had been an artist. She had died young. The studio was exactly as it was on the last day she had worked in it before her fatal illness; tools lying around and uncompleted work on the benches; sad indeed.

Two mornings later, I was requested to feed a couple of bed-patients who were not allowed the use of cutlery. Entering the first sideroom with a bowl of porridge, I sat down in the chair at his bedside. One spoonful, then another, and after the third mouthful – he waved the spoon away indignantly and sat up straight-looking at me with great contempt in his eyes, calling out, "Don't you feel ashamed of yourself young man, feeding me with that muck; put it in the swill bin and bring me a bacon sandwich or else I'll smash your face in!"

Unable to control myself I began laughing in sheer delight at the unexpected vitriolic outburst; but this only aggravated him further. Suddenly raising his head away from the backrest he reached out behind him and grabbing a pillow – walloped me with it, which resulted in the porridge bowl flying across the floor:

"You stupid bastard," he bawled out, "If I get out of this bed I will knock the silly grin off your bloody face."

At that moment, one of the female nurses entered the room and began scolding him, "Mr Johnson! – I'm terribly ashamed of you. This is no way to behave to someone who has come here specially to attend to you. Now then, what have you to say for yourself?"

The old man winced and appeared as though he was attempting to shrink into the bed. "He's come to look after me has he? I'm sorry nurse," said he, apologising to her, and sounding as though he meant to cry. At this, she sat on the bed and put her arms around him and comforted him, as she did so, he slyly peered at me in triumph. I cleared up the mess, then brought him a bacon sandwich which he gratefully received; and though his gums were furnished with only three nicotine-stained teeth, he tore into the sandwich with the gusto of a famished wolf. When the female nurse left the room, he ceased chewing for a moment to mutter, "The next time you bring bloody porridge to me, young man, I'll bounce the basin off your head, see if you can grin then. Don't forget, I pay your wages, you ignorant bugger."

"And I'm grateful to you, sir, for doing so," said I before leaving him.

The next sideroom patient welcomed me warmly; and proved instantly that he possessed a healthy appetite for anything he considered edible. I had learned previously that flowers were never placed on his locker for that very reason.

Joe was an escape risk; this factor alone proved that his mental faculties were not completely institutionalised. There was no relaxed strolling in the grounds for him; like some condemned prisoner destined for the gallows, he had a small high-walled courtyard to himself. Backwards and forwards, round and round, pacing relentlessly as though determined to work off his surplus nervous energy, and sounding and looking like some proud angry plaintiff, appealing to the Gods. When he was blowing off steam, one could be excused for believing that he was a violent man, someone to keep a distance from for fear he may fell you with one blow from his huge fist. The truth was, he would really have to be provoked before giving a thought to use of violence.

One afternoon I entered the courtyard to engage him in conversation. "Hello Joe. I've brought you some fags!" Cigarettes and sweets were his only luxuries. Given the opportunity I reckon he would have smoked himself to death; but then I considered that no proud and spirited big cat, hauled from its own natural environment, could have been more bored to death in its narrow cage than poor Joe was in his courtyard. I assumed it was for his own health's sake that his tobacco was doled out to him. Then again, no interested party wishes to lose a private fee-paying patient through any cause whatever, for it is bad economics. Though when dealing with institutional boredom in patients like Joe, the question could be asked, which is the lesser evil, a few more cigarettes, or more potent tranquilizers?

"What's wrong with Tyneside, then, is there no more work up there again?" he enquired after I had provided him with a light.

"Yes, there's work to be had Joe; but I prefer being in the South," I replied.

"Do you like working in these places?" he asked, after taking a couple of draws on his fag.

"Yes, Joe. I get great satisfaction from this type of work; I've worked in a number of hospitals now, public ones; and it's a steady job."

"Do you take a drink, Geordie?" There was a kind of longing in his voice and in his eyes when he asked the question.

"I like a couple of pints Joe. I'll be having a drink tonight on my way home," said I.

"I wish I could join you, Geordie, I would be no bother – this is not living, Geordie, it's worse than prison; I've got nothing to look forward to. If I was in prison, at least I could look forward to my release some day."

"I wish to hell I could take you for a couple of pints, Joe; I know you wouldn't be any bother," said I earnestly, even though I wasn't familiar with his case papers. I had met many such patients like Joe, who made themselves mentally ill, from sheer frustration, boredom, and total absence of hope.

"I don't know what went wrong with me, Geordie. My family told me I would be put right once I agreed to come into hospital – the bastards – they tricked me. The only treatment I've had in here is bloody tablets; this bloody place!" The poor fellow was beginning to become agitated. "Bastards. Curse them – curse them."

He took to walking round his pen again, his speed and his curses increasing by the second; he was off on one of his journeys of self-torment. I discreetly withdrew back into the ward. He much preferred being alone during his outbursts, which could last for fifteen minutes or more, and which left him exhausted. There would be no purpose in my remaining with him. I could not help him with his problems; who could? The drug researchers in the field of psychiatric medicine have, in the past few years, come up with some new amazing discoveries. The main drawback with most of them is that their effect is of a limited period, and therefore the patient has to continue taking the medicine, for they are solely suppression drugs; and whether such drugs can be prescribed for any individual patient on a permanent basis without resulting in serious side-effects, only time will tell!

Apart from individuals like Joe, who would never be reconciled to their loss of liberty, life for the average patient in this private asylum was more agreeable than that experienced by the majority in the large over-crowded public institutions. One factor I observed, and which surprised me, was to discover that despite their being incarcerated in a mental hospital, they had some access to their capital. If someone fancied a new book, new shoes, a box of cigars, etc., they got their favourite nurse to do the shopping for them. Nor were they past attempting to bribe that nurse for some favour to be done for them. Though it was my first experience in a private mental hospital, I was aware from my reading, that conditions here, as in the public mental hospitals, had changed for the better!

In the past, conditions even for the private patient who suffered from behaviour problems must have been grim. When one learns of the cruel treatment meted out to King George III during his recurrent bouts of insanity, then no one ought to be amazed at the vicious treatment that was inflicted upon lesser mortals, whether pauper, or private lunatics. I couldn't imagine violence being inflicted on any patients in this hospital; the nursing staff adhered strictly to the letter of their mental nursing rule book; patience and a sense of humour prevailed, in place of the back-hander or the fist. Though I must add that the lack of imagination was obvious. Institutional boredom still prevailed here for the majority of the patients! What I did find interesting and even amusing in this private hospital, was to observe the attitudes of some of the patients towards certain members of the staff; mentally ill, they may be, but their outlook was in no way diminished. If their requests were not attended to instantly, or if they were crossed, however inadvertently, they were not slow to remind us that they paid our salaries, and that we should do as we were told. Their communications were always on a master-to-servant level. This factor alone proved that unlike their long-term brethren in the public mental hospitals, their individuality had not been suppressed. They were not seeking equality with staff, on the contrary, as far as they were concerned the boot was on the other foot. Even their phantasms appeared to be tainted with middle-class morality!

The Head Nurse was a fine fellow to work alongside, though of the reserved type. As far as discussion of patient records was concerned, only he and the doctor, had access to the case papers; all I could ever observe was the daily report books that were kept on the ward. However, my past experiences held me in good stead and I felt sure my observations were reasonably accurate. Though there was no doubt that the inmates in this hospital were affluent and able to secure more of the comforts of life, like their more unfortunate brethren in the public institutions, they still had each other to contend with! Communal living, and all it implies, is an ideal breeding ground for contemptuous and often provocative behaviour. At least that has been my observation in the mental institutions, and the large overcrowded common-lodging houses I had frequented whilst on the road.

March 1962 was drawing to a close, and Kathy and I once more packed our bags; this time to Hammersmith, London, to take up employment as nursing assistants in a private residential home for the elderly.

A Private Home for the Elderly

A part from the domestic staff, another couple were employed as nursing assistants, and between the four of us, we were responsible for covering the day shifts; the night nurse was non-resident. The proprietor himself acted as cook, as well as supervisor. His wife was performing similar roles in another of their establishments in the same neighbourhood.

It was quite a large house, the top floor being occupied by the resident staff. All the other floors, excepting the ground floor where the common rooms were situated, and the basement where the kitchen and sculleries were to be found, were given over to bedrooms.

At seven o'clock on our first morning, Kathy and I took over the early shift, and the early tea-round. In Biggleswade, where I had met Kathy, in the home for the aged, the Master and Matron insisted upon a reasonable amount of ventilation in the sleeping dormitories, whatever the weather; and providing the bedding is adequate, then fresh air is to the benefit of all concerned.

However, I presumed that in a private residential home where the fees are pretty stiff, a certain amount of leeway has to be allowed in some directions. In a bedroom where five aged people are lodged, and only one of them desires to have the window open at night, then that individual loses out; that is democracy, so I'm told. Now in my time, I have kipped in stables, and in doss houses, so I cannot be accused of over-sensitivity when I state that on entering the first bedroom with a tray laden with cups of tea, I hurriedly placed the tray on the top of a locker and flew out of the room, to place my head out of a window on the landing; to be followed by Kathy in the same plight. After that experience I learned to hold my breath whenever I was on early morning tea round! In all fairness, one has to consider that when this establishment had been a private house, each of these bedrooms would have most probably contained only one bed, and two people in it at the most. Now, there were five beds, and practically no vacant space between each one; and this crush-situation prevailed in the ladies' bedrooms also. How on earth some of these old dears would have got out of the building in an emergency made me shudder, for in my opinion it would have been impossible. Yet I supposed that this

Home, not unlike the large overcrowded lodging hostels I had slept in many a night, had been visited by the appropriate Fire Inspectors, and passed as satisfactory! Like Alice in Wonderland, I too was bemused: very little was as it appeared or ought to be.

There was one credit to the Governor, he could cook, and the meals provided were decent; though he took some persuading that I possessed an appetite three or four times larger than most of the elderly residents. His own appetite was meagre; but as I pointed out to him, that was due in my opinion to his craving for tobacco. One afternoon whilst he and I were sitting alone in the kitchen having a cup of tea, he began talking discreetly about the benefits of running such a concern as his.

"It's money for old rope, Thomas. Get yourself a large house on mortgage; get your business cards distributed to all the doctors in the area where you intend to start off; and providing you are willing to work hard at the beginning, you never look back. As soon as I paid off this mortgage, I took on another house, and my wife runs it. You'd be surprised at the demand for such places in a big city like London. Most of the residents in here have been boarded out by their families, who are either professional people and haven't got the time to look after their parents; or by sons, or daughters, who can't be bothered to have them on their hands."

"So you would suggest if I had the means, to get into the business?" I asked; realising that was what he was after telling me.

"Of course, man; it's the thing to do. You're just the man for such work with the experience you have behind you," said he encouragingly!

Before setting up business in this obviously lucrative market of looking after other people's parents, grandmas and grandfathers, the Governor and his wife had owned a corner shop dealing in groceries; a business, which in my humble opinion they were more suited for.

Until I entered this particular home, I would not have believed that some old folks could be as selfish, and as mischievous as children; perhaps I was naive after all. I was amazed one afternoon to witness two elderly adults, still in control of their mental faculties, begin squabbling fiercely over who sat in a particular armchair in the common room; and it was only my swift intervention that prevented them from indulging in fisticuffs. And the choice of television programmes was another daily issue which could often create a rise in tempers.

Visiting time was also an interesting psychological experience!

Many of the visitors arrived loaded up with packages: biscuits, cakes, chocolates and fruit and soft drinks. They greeted their particular resident in a hearty style, as though they were arriving home from the office; or from shopping; or perhaps the theatre dressing rooms: "Hello Darling. Had a lovely day? Sorry I'm late. I've brought you something you always like." Whilst their loved one sampled the goodies, the visitor, appearing slightly ill-at-ease, shrouded him or herself in tobacco smoke; the ensuing conversation sounded stiff and pompous.

It soon became apparent that certain residents had been bringing Kathy and myself to the attention of their relatives, or friends; as a result, before departing, those visitors concerned would call us aside and discreetly press upon us small tokens of gratitude for looking after their loved ones so well; as they claimed.

The gifts were often chocolates for Kathy, and cigars for me, though I was a fervent non-smoker; and sometimes cash to both of us. I was surprised by all this, for during all my hospital experience I always refrained from showing favouritism to any individual patient; I treated them all alike; simply in the fashion I would wish and expect to be treated by those who were employed to attend to my own welfare. However, I realised it would appear an offence to those generous folks if we were to refuse their gifts, so we accepted them in the spirit they were offered. Indeed I hoped that perhaps one day, one of those kind individuals would decide to be more generous, or display more eccentricity, and present me with a good sized cheque; for I too would love to be affluent, I have been poor too long.

Though the majority of the residents appeared to be coping, and adjusting in some measure to the strange experience of communal-living, there were a few of them, I observed, who were in my estimation, beginning to display personality changes! I pondered whether many had entered the Home by choice; most had in some way been pressurised into accepting exile from their former and more congenial surroundings. I often thought of poor Joe, in Bedford, who had claimed he'd been tricked into entering the Asylum.

Such was the demand for places in these establishments, in this affluent capital of ours; that though the majority of the residents displayed a patronising tolerance towards those belonging to a lower social rank than themselves (the staff), they were always cautious in their attitudes towards the Governor – there was always a waiting list for beds.

Personally, I would sooner have been regarded as being a little potty, and be incarcerated in the small private Bedlam in Bedford, than spend the evening of my life in some private city Home, where the main motivation was profit.

Six weeks was more than sufficient for Kathy to tolerate there. And so we left one morning without any fixed abode to go to. Lodging our suitcases in a railway luggage office, we set off to search for a furnished room.

Life in a Public House

I believe it was my past futile experiences of room-hunting in London that decided me to explore Croydon for lodgings. During our hunt, we came across a public house with a card in its window advertising for resident staff.

"With a bit of luck dear, this is where we put-up, until we find more suitable accommodation. We may as well have an employer as our landlord. Now don't forget Kathy, leave the talking to me."

The manager, a shrimp-like character, whose countenance resembled a pictorial for rough cider, appeared impressed by my supposed public house record, gained mainly from keen observation on the right side of the counter with a pint glass in my hand. I deemed it wise to admit that Kathy was inexperienced, but very adaptable.

"Can you both start work this evening?" he asked, rather anxiously after the interview.

"Sure we can, sir. We'll go and bring our luggage and settle in right away," I replied; and pleased to do so; far better to earn money than spend on high rents.

At four o'clock the same afternoon, having just unloaded our cases, there was a gentle tap on our room door. "Come in," I called out. The other resident barman entered with a loaded up tray, which he placed on the table.

"I've brought the afternoon tea for the three of us. I used to bring it up for the other couple that left; we always had it together," said he rather appealingly.

"That's fine," said I. "My name is Tom; this is my wife Kathy."

After we had all shaken hands, Kathy played host.

"My name is Harry," said he, accepting a cup of tea. "Did the Boss tell you no drinking or smoking on duty?" he enquired.

"He did, Harry. Though he also mentioned we could have a drink on our break," replied I. "As regards tobacco, neither of us smoke, thankfully," I added deliberately, as a hint that I would not sanction anyone smoking in our quarters.

"The second manager is the best; that's the big fellow," said Harry. "When the Boss and his wife have their day off, the under-manager lets us have a drink; just one of course, but you can pay for your own after that, so long as you can hold it of course. Have you been in the trade long, Tom?" Harry enquired.

"A fair time, Harry. Long enough to know the pitfalls," said I.

"We get a lot of darkies in here, West Indians I think. The boss and his wife don't like the blacks – Do you like darkies Tom?" asked Harry, sounding curious.

"I don't find the colour of anyone's skin a problem, Harry; I judge people solely on their social behaviour. Those who dislike coloured people ought to lodge their complaints with God, he created them," said I, though conscious that Kathy did not share my views. Harry began laughing with his mouth full of cake and he was spitting it out in all directions, much to the disgust of Kathy.

"I've never looked at it that way before," said Harry. "Blacks don't bother me, there's good and bad in every race," he added.

At 5.30 in the evening, Harry and I opened the pub doors and retired behind the counter of the large saloon bar. Kathy was in the select room – along with the under manager. I felt confident she would be content working alongside him, though how she would get along with the boss's wife, when she came down, was another matter. I had urged her to be cool, and give us time to find another nursing post which we would seek, as soon as we could find a more suitable address to apply from.

It being a Monday evening, the first customers were mainly men on their way home from work. By seven o'clock the saloon began filling up, and the under-manager came through and joined Harry and myself. The governor, although working in the select room with his wife and Kathy, kept flitting from one part of the house to the other, serving, and also keeping a sharp eye on both the customers, and the staff. At breaktime I pulled myself a pint, paid for it, and went into the cubbyhole to enjoy it. Kathy followed me with a cup of coffee; releasing a sigh as she sat down beside me.

"How are you getting on with Snow White?" I enquired, referring to the manageress.

"She's all right up to now. Though as I expected, she keeps quizzing me whenever we have a slack moment: what have I worked at in the past? How long have we been married, and whether we have any children?"

"Listen to me dear. Whenever anyone shows too much interest into your own affairs, fill their heads with nonsense; that is what they really want, so don't disappoint them. The next time she quizzes you tell her that my grandfather was an Irish Papal Count; and was married to a great granddaughter of Rip Van Winkle. She'll ignore you then," said I with a smile.

"What! I'm not going to talk like that to her – she'll think I'm drunk," she responded.

"Snow White and that man of hers will ensure you don't get drunk in their time," I remarked dryly.

Despite my being on the wrong side of the counter, serving in place of drinking, I was finding the experience interesting, observing individuals enter for their first drink of the evening and appearing their normal selves, then, as the evening progressed, along with their intake of liquor, I was able to note the changes developing – not only in their behaviour, but in their faces! In some of the customers, a kind of Jekyll-to-Hyde transformation appeared to be taking place within; these are the characters who could create the biggest headache eventually, unless handled correctly. The most harmless characters, on study, were those who were simply degenerating into fools, the more they drank; once led outside and told to go home, they inevitably walk away after a feeble protest that they are still sober! Whenever, during the evening, one or two of the coloured chaps reacted strongly to the governor's obvious contempt towards them, he did not back away from them, despite being small and of light stature. I, for one, was determined to remain neutral; I was there to serve as a barman, not a chucker-out. A little more tact from the boss would have more served the purpose!

It was 11.20 p.m. by the time we got the last dismayed customer off the premises and secured the doors. The governor pulled a pint for Harry and myself and a light ale for Kathy, and the three of us went upstairs, leaving the other three to tot up the night's takings. The pub was situated on the High Street, and as luck would have it our bedroom overlooked it, so despite the warm weather we were obliged to close the window, for outside the usual late-night boozy debates, arguments, and attempts at singing were in full chorus, with not a policeman in sight. The management, the crafty lot, had their bedrooms at the rear of the building where it was as silent as the grave.

Eight o'clock next morning, a gentle tap on our bedroom door; I sensed it was Harry, playing his usual part of butler:

"Come on in, Harry, the door is unlocked," I called out, as I sat up in bed. He entered with tea and biscuits on a tray.

"Harry, pal," I began in a grateful tone, "if my rich Uncle, who lives up North, were to die, and remember me in his will, I would offer you the post of valet and housekeeper, would you accept it?"

"You bet I would mate; providing you kept a good cellar and allowed me free access to it at all times," replied he.

When he departed I got out of bed and poured out the tea.

"Why don't you tell Harry to stay in his own room," remarked Kathy, as she accepted the tea. "We don't want him coming in here morning and night."

I sat on the bed and gazed at her, amused. "You mean I ought to insult him after he's good enough to do us these good turns? Can't you sense the man is lonely and is only seeking companionship. Anyway, it's time we were up, we have to be downstairs by eight-thirty."

"If he's lonely why don't he get married then?" she asked.

"I can't answer that one; perhaps he's after the boss's wife," I replied with a straight face.

"No one but her husband would have that bitch," said she dismissively.

When we got downstairs breakfast was waiting for us, cooked by the manager's wife, who even smiled on greeting us good-morning. As the days went by, I realised that both the manager and his wife had taken to me! Yet somehow I was not surprised to learn this, for oddly enough such dyspeptic-looking individuals, whom everyone seemed to fear, or despise, in most of my previous occupations had taken to me like to a son and had shown favours to me. I concluded that it was because I always dealt with such acidy creatures in a respectful, and humorous fashion; it was my long-held opinion that it cost nothing to coax anyone suffering from such an indisposition, for I believe they are more to be pitied than scorned!

If their consideration towards me was considered a bounty, it certainly didn't please Kathy. As regarding Harry, he was too intent on employing every opportunity to have a sly drink during working hours, to concern himself how he was thought of by his employers! I had observed that whenever the saloon bar was busy, Harry made it a policy to have at least two half-pints of beer posted at various points along the counter and always near some group of drinkers – who sensing Harry's ploy, were ever ready to claim ownership of the drink, if ever the crafty governor made any comment about it. My own tactics were different. I would periodically make some excuse to go down to the cellar, have a pint direct from one of the barrels, using one of the enamel jugs kept down there, then I would return up to the saloon with a crate of bottled beer. It was essential for both Harry and myself, light sleepers, to have a few pints every night if we were to get any sleep, with the noise outside on the High Street.

The change of atmosphere when the governor and his wife were absent on their day off was remarkable; even Kathy, who really disliked the work, was completely relaxed under the supervision of the big, jovial under-manager. The West Indian lads were on their best behaviour for no one upset them. Broad smiles gleamed on their dusky faces; even those who had been barred strolled cautiously in, and were welcomed by all. Twice during the evening the under-manager allowed us a drink on the house, and Harry and I would pretend we had been gasping for it, much to the amusement of those customers observant enough to know that both of us were getting our share. But three weeks of pint-pulling was quite sufficient for Kathy, and I had to agree with her. We no sooner moved into a furnished room, than we applied for posts as nursing assistants at the Cheshire Home in Ampthill, Bedfordshire; and were successful!

The Cheshire Home

The Home was situated on land owned, I believe, by the Duke of Bedford; and the surrounding country scenery was a tonic after our dismal stay in London.

Apart from the sleeping quarters, I was pleased to observe the natural integration of the sexes which went a long way, in my opinion, to create the social harmony that obviously prevailed. Indeed such democracy was even extended to the staff side, for not only did we work together, but had our meals together: the Matron, the Warden and his wife, the nursing staff, the cooks and the domestics, all sat at one long table.

Where ever you go you're sure to find a Geordie! In my own case, another Geordie. I was greeted by one within minutes of entering the male ward on my first morning. He came hurriedly up to me in his wheelchair, calling out at the top of his voice the instant he heard me greeting everyone with a good morning.

"Hey man, have' yet browt any stotty cake, or leek puddin' with yeh, from Geordie-land."

"If yeh divint stop shouting bonny lad, I'll bring the Pollis, to yeh," I retorted. And the sound of another Geordie voice brought tears to his eyes. He told me that of the few rare visitors he got, none of them were Geordies.

One important thing, that all the residents treasured, was their independence; and to witness some of them insisting on dressing themselves, and even shaving unaided, was a valuable lesson indeed. One particular man, who spent most of his time in bed, apart from two hours during the day sitting in an armchair, and was absolutely crippled as a result of rheumatoid arthritis, struggled to shave himself, yet there was no doubt in my mind he was suffering hell silently in so doing.

I was determined to relieve him of the agonising chore, and the only way to do so was to prove in his presence that I was an efficient barber with literally hundreds of shaves and haircuts, to my credit. Within a week he surrendered to me that part of his misguided independence! I learned from him that since becoming afflicted with his crippling and most painful disease he had been injected with every conceivable arthritis-combative drug there was on the market, besides swallowing numerous courses of tablets, all without success. In the beginning he had spent quite a sum of money going the rounds of the known specialists. Now he was resigned; and cynical. His cynicism, of course was directed not against the medical fraternity who had primed his system with all those drugs in the hope that one of them may create a favourable reaction; no, his anger was directed against that inevitable factor known as fate!

Sam, as I shall call him, was also sick to death of having to resort to the nightly dose of sleeping tablets, without which his nights would be similar to his days: long and weary, lying gazing up to the ceiling, and attempting not to concentrate on his lot.

One morning as I was shaving him, he whispered, "Tom, would you bring me a quarter bottle of whisky when you go out this afternoon on your walk?" I was on a split-shift that day.

"Yes of course I will Sam," said I, knowing that he intended to dispense with his usual nightly sedation. Which was the worse for him in the long run, whisky or drugs, I know not, but on considering his age and his permanent infirmity, I didn't intend to lecture on it.

"Don't let anyone see you pass it on to me, Tom, I don't want any bother over it," he continued whispering.

"I won't Sam. But I shouldn't worry about it if I were you. Surely you're aware that a number of the residents take a drink, and all the staff seem to enjoy a drop; I know the Italian staff drink their share of wine; Paddy likes his Guinness; the Warden and his wife take a drink; I don't know about the Matron, but I guess she likes a drop; and Kathy and I take a drink."

Does a smile always portray inner contentment? Does laughter always express inner joy? I often pondered whether it was a display of sheer bravado when I beheld such gaiety and exuberance among the majority of residents, especially those confined to bed, or those unable to move about without the aid of crutches, sticks, or wheelchair! I well remember one evening watching a television programme in the lounge called *Come Dancing*. I was observing the faces of the residents – especially the ladies – who seemed in a sense to feel they were in that particular ballroom, sitting on the sidelines, just waiting to be asked up on to the floor; for all of them were dressed for the occasion! Though of course, this dressing up business on an evening, after having spent the day occupied with their own particular craft or hobby, was mainly to appear attractive to one another. It was only natural that being confined to a restricted environment, these men and women who sought romance, young or old, had to seek it within their own surroundings. Some of the young women were really bonny lasses, and some of the young men were equally hand-some, therefore it was a fertile environment for the normal competition between the sexes; and of course the inevitable display of jealousy, and lovers' tiffs.

Apart from the complete integration of the sexes, which was important, I think the main reason for the apparent contentment of the majority of the residents for most of the time was their acceptance of their disabilities and agreeing to live with them; not forgetting the easy-going conditions promoted by all concerned. Equally important to each resident capable of managing, was the fact they had a daily week-day routine occupation, something to look forward to on the usual working days, Monday to Friday. In the beginning each new resident was assessed for any natur-al talent they may possess. If one discovered a talent for art, then they were encour-aged to take it up; though the final choice was theirs. They could choose a craft: leather goods; basket making; clock and watch repairs; the choice was reasonably extensive. Those individuals confined to bed were not forgotten; providing they possessed the use of their hands they too could follow the arts or crafts. It was a common sense environment; and no doubt kept at a distance institutional boredom, and the inevitable issuing of tranquilising drugs.

Sam must have been pretty well off! He was now having his whisky every day; even offering to pay me for bringing it, though I refused. He also had his own house, despite having been urged to sell it. He lived in the hope, so he told me, that someone like myself and Kathy, would come along some day, befriend him, as we had done, and take him home and look after him. He offered to pay us the same wages as we were then receiving, leave the house to us in his will; and even declared he would have me initiated into Freemasonry, of which he himself was a member! Well, I had no inclination to become a member of any secret association; but his other offers were certainly generous. However, I had to confide in him that I had been a life-long drifter; and so would not dream of taking on such responsi-bility.

For a while now, Kathy had been complaining to me that the work was proving too heavy for her, and sadly I had no other option but to agree with her! As far as physical work is concerned, nursing in a mental hospital is a picnic when compared to the tending of the severely physically handicapped, for despite the aid of modern lifting equipment, there is still such heavy work to do; obesity is another of the curs-es that afflict those who are almost totally immobile.

In October, we left, and travelled to Nottingham. Within hours of arriving, we had found comfortable accommodation in the house of a widow, an elderly Jewish lady, in a select part of the city. And a week later, Kathy went to work in one of the mental hospitals, whilst I began in another, a short distance away.

Christmas 1962, I believe, was one of the happiest I ever had – a really old-fashioned one: dinner in the best room of the house, in the company of our landlady, her son and his wife; the evening spent around the piano and the singing of carols, plus good wine. The family were Christian Jews, hence Christmas was spent in the usual seasonal spirit; she was a fine, kind, refined lady, who possessed a good sense of humour; she was in need of it, when I began to sing carols in my well-trained bathroom-style Italian!

The Epileptic Colony

Come March the following year, 1963, I was becoming impatient to move on. So was Kathy, but her idea was a double post, in private service, which I wanted nothing to do with. Nonetheless she went ahead scanning the vacancy columns of *The Times*, and *The Lady*; convinced I would submit. Meanwhile I was looking elsewhere; and hoping I would get my hands on the morning post first! Eventually I applied for a nursing position in an Institution for the Welfare of Epileptics. Now working in mental hospitals had acquainted me with the malady of Epilepsy from the beginning; however, I realised that to work in a colony that cared exclusively for the sufferer would be a rewarding experience. On being successful in my application, I served my notice, unknown to Kathy; and one morning after she had left for work, I pulled out, and made my way to the colony, which was situated in Lancashire.

As a boy, I had observed at various times a number of individuals suffering fits, in the schoolyard, on the main terrace in my neighbourhood, and sometimes in the public parks. Like most children I was both attracted and disturbed by the experiences. At such an early age I was unaware that there were different kinds of seizures, or various causes for them. I suppose I must have heard the term epilepsy used to differentiate between one fit and another, though it would mean nothing to me then. However, those early distressful scenes of people having fits appeared not to have clouded my judgment, or common-sense; I must have been totally devoid of such primitive instincts as superstition! As I had never from the beginning held any prejudice towards those suffering from mental illness, likewise I have never been inflicted with the ignorance and superstition which is commonly held towards those suffering from epilepsy.

The moment I entered the ward on my first morning, I sensed I was under mass-scrutiny; some of them stared at me critically; others gazed at me solely through curiosity; only two or three of them bid me good morning in answer to my own greetings. There was no disguising the familiar institutional attitude of the majority of residents towards a new member of staff; as far as they were concerned, I would be placed on probation for a time. But then I was used to it. Within seconds, all the usual early morning institutional activities recommenced, some dressing, others making their way towards the washroom; a few becoming engaged in the seemingly unavoidable early morning polemics; two of them in particular were flushed in self-agitation and appeared liable to erupt into violence. At that moment one of the established nurses walked by these two, completely ignoring the argument taking place. While I was pondering over the apparent lack of discipline, the Charge Nurse, came barging out of his office, and after giving me a critical look, grabbed both antagonists by the scruff of the neck, threatening them with bed if they didn't pipe down. He called me aside, and told me I wasn't to stand by and watch patients about to fight each other. I was of the opinion that the other nurse who had ignored the fracas, and who was senior to myself, ought to have stepped in; but I refrained from mentioning it, instead I commented that it would be poor psychology for myself to behave in an authoritative manner within minutes of entering the ward for the first time.

This explanation didn't suit him; he peered at my dryly, before retorting, "I hope you haven't come here solely to study psychology!"

I smiled broadly at his exhibition of wit, before replying, "No sir, I've come here to work. Though I'm not against employing psychology, or tact, if the term is more suitable."

"All right. Go into the washroom and keep an eye on things," said he in a more conciliatory manner.

In the washroom, the problems, mainly created by a large number of men competing for the use of the small number of washbasins, reminded me of the many large common-lodging houses I had frequented when on the road. Certainly the present atmosphere in this washroom bore no comparison to that of the mental institutions I had worked in, where discipline was the sacred rule. I had to remind myself that despite the hierarchical structure of this institution appearing identical to that of the mental hospitals, the patients in this colony were not altogether subdued; and though some of them were obviously suffering from personality problems, they were not certified patients. I had to realise they were undergoing a programme of long-term treatment under medical supervision, hopefully, in order to bring about effective control of their seizures! So I supposed that in this institution, co-operation was gained on a give and take basis; I had yet to find out.

After breakfast, in the company of another nurse, we accompanied those who worked in the gardens, everyone mucking-in, no idle supervisors. At ten o'clock, two of the patients went off to collect the mid-morning coffee. We sat down to enjoy it; those who smoked lit up; a few curious ones began quizzing me: Where had I come from? What was it like to work in a mental hospital? Was I married? What surprised me was the apparent camaraderie being displayed towards me by some of those who earlier on in the morning had been clearly antagonistic. I could only conclude that being away from the close and overcrowded confines of the ward had the usual beneficial effects I had often observed in other institutions: temperaments were mellowed.

The patients were having lunch when the Matron, who incidentally was the first male I had known to hold such office, entered the ward in the company of a burly-looking man. Another nurse standing beside me whispered that this was the Medical Superintendent, and he had once been in charge of Rampton Top Security Hospital. To my surprise, he inquired of the patients whether they had any complaints. I observed the Charge Nurse peering a little apprehensively around the tables, as though half expecting someone to break the silence that had followed the arrival of the visitors. But the request was met with a mixture of awe and suspicion, and I wondered whether this was the first time such a request had been made! In the past, I had been present a number of times on wards in various mental hospitals, when the Superintendent had paid a surprise visit, but never had any one of them invited comments from the patients. Perhaps, I thought, the patients here assumed the remark was an empty gesture; or if some of them did believe it was genuine, then no one had the courage to break ranks. Then again, perhaps there were no complaints to make. I had previously met the Matron; now I was introduced to the Superintendent. His sharp-looking eyes peered into mine as we shook hands.

"You're a Geordie, I understand! Good stock from that part of the country," he commented in a quiet voice, before strolling off into the ward office along with the Matron and Charge Nurse. The table-talk resumed, though in a more hushed tone. Suddenly there was a strangled cry from a far table near the wall and a chair fell over along with the patient who had occupied it, the cry now taking the form of a high-pitched scream.

"I expected as much," remarked a colleague, as we moved toward the victim, "every time we have some bugger come in from the office, someone throws a fit."

I moved the chair aside whilst the other nurse attended to the patient who by now was jerking violently. The other patients continued with their meal; no doubt they didn't wish to concentrate on an incident which only reminded them of their own malady. By now the Charge Nurse, accompanied by the Matron and Superintendent, were on the scene. The patient began recovering, and the matron took his pulse, then ordered me and another nurse to assist him to a sofa so as he could lie down. But he resisted, and rose – unsupported, even making a move to resume his meal at table, "Lie down; you can finish your lunch later," demanded the Charge Nurse. But still the patient resisted – and attempted to resume his place at the table. I knew from past experiences that no institutional Charge Nurse will tolerate having his orders challenged or ignored; I assumed the presence of the Superintendent may be holding him back; but yet again, I had never heard of any Medical Director questioning the authority of a Charge Nurse on the subject of ward discipline. However, it was the Superintendent himself, who in a quiet, steel-like firmness, commanded, "Do as you're told and lie down!" And it was the Superintendent who took him over to the sofa; which the patient concerned was in need of, for within minutes of lying down he was snoring loudly.

Apart from work in the fields, there were various occupations which kept the patients busy during normal working day hours from Monday to Friday; woodwork, handicrafts, boot repairs, and other tasks; far more rewarding than having to sit in the dayrooms, gazing into space, and getting on each other's nerves. In the evenings there were also various pastimes: snooker, table-tennis, chess, draughts, books, radio and television. Not many patients appeared to sit around like zombies; indeed they were encouraged to occupy themselves, for activity is the enemy of epilepsy!

I was having a game of snooker on the staff billiard table one morning on a rest day, for half a crown stake, when the Matron entered the room; calling me aside, he whispered that he had my wife in his office, and wished me to proceed there after the game. I felt embarrassed, for I had never admitted in my application that I had a wife. Needless to say, I lost my half-crown stake. When I entered the matron's office, Kathy and he were having coffee. I soon learned that this gentleman would have been quite qualified as a Marriage Guidance Officer, had he decided to look in that direction; and he immediately got to work on me. But, I was only too willing to be convinced and was soon won over.

"Now, as I see it, Nurse Callaghan, I don't wish to lose you; so as your wife has told me she has had nursing experience I have suggested she joins us here. Of course we can't offer you joint accommodation, but leave it with me; let us see how things work out, then I'm confident we shall find you something suitable soon."

I was surprised to learn that Kathy had arrived, complete with her luggage; it was obvious to me she must have communicated with the Matron prior to her arrival, and been offered employment. How on earth she had discovered my whereabouts she refused to tell me, other than commenting, "I worked the oracle, darling!"

"Are you by chance, any relation to the late Sherlock Holmes?" I asked her. She only smiled, wisely. "Never mind, you're here now, that is all that matters; I was going to send for you soon!" I added, hoping I sounded convincing. I assisted her with the large suitcases she had brought, which to judge by the weight of them must have contained scrap metal. The female nurses' block was a distance away from the male quarters.

"I don't care for the living arrangements, Tom; we'll never be able to get together!" said she.

"I know different, my love," said I smiling; "there are at least three male nurses I know of who creep here most nights, and I shall join their ranks." It appeared a comfortable room; certainly the bed looked in good fettle. I sat down in the armchair, and offered her some advice about the work she was about to take on.

"Now, listen to me carefully, Kathy. You will find this work a little different to nursing in the mental hospitals. Point one: the patients, are not certified. Some of them are very temperamental, however; they're not to blame; so don't say anything or do anything to upset them. Don't be bossy; take it steady until you become acquainted with their moods and ways!"

Two weeks later she had to have a few stitches to her face, after one of her patients had thrown a cup at her. She came to my room quite upset, and complained to me, "It's no different here to working in a mental hospital; you told me they were not mental."

"I told you, Kathy, that epilepsy has nothing to do with mental illness as such; but I warned you, that for some of them their disorder does create personal problems which can result in some of them becoming extremely agitated at times. Just be cautious dear, and tactful. And bear in mind Kathy, there are far more complicated people living outside this colony than in it."

It was a fine April evening as we walked up the country road towards the pub situated at the top of the hill, and which was now our local; the people were friendly, and the beer and the music and singing were beneficial to well-being.

"I wish we could go and live in Bedford, and settle down," remarked Kathy, suddenly, looking at me speculatively for any signs of response. But I refrained from comment, apart from remarking how springtime alters the landscape for the better. "We both had jobs, and were together when we first met; and I had a house," she continued. "All this moving around gets us nowhere; we're no better than tinkers." There were tears in her eyes as she spoke; and I felt uncomfortable, for I knew she was unhappy.

"If we were to return to Bedford, where would we live? It would have to be in bed-sitter-land; two people living in one room is not a good choice; I had more than enough of such conditions when I was a kid," said I; making any excuse to bring the discussion to an end.

"My sister would put us up, Tom, if we went to Biggleswade," said she, her eyes lighting up in anticipation.

"All right dear, I've got the message, I shall think about it," said I, as we arrived at the pub.

By now I was aware of those patients who usually had fits during the day; those who could have them any time of the day or night; and the few, who had their seizures at night whilst asleep. When my turn of night-duty came round, I was fully aware that I would have to be more alert in this colony than I had needed to be in the mental hospital. Each seizure had to be noted and booked, for such information could be a factor in deciding whether any unusual symptoms were being revealed and which could point in turn to possible side-effects from the anti-convulsant drugs being administered. There appeared to be no opportunity of putting our feet up; the risk was perhaps too great. Even a patient getting out of bed to go to the toilet had to be discreetly observed until back in bed; falling onto concrete toilet floors can create more than a headache; nevertheless there are those who resent having their footsteps dogged. Another routine to be carried out on night-duty was to go round the sleeping dormitory at various times and ensure there was no one having a seizure; also to observe whether it was possible to detect if a patient was having a nightmare and if so, gently rouse him, for such dreams promote panic, and panic is one of the factors which precipitate a seizure. If a fit lasted more than five minutes, or if a second one, followed immediately after the first, then I had to get the senior nurse, it was his responsibility to decide whether to call the doctor out of his bed. But these active nights were no bother to me, I had always been one of the fortunate ones who could sleep as well during the day. But I was always pleased when my night-stint came to an end, especially during spring, or summer for I am an outdoor man.

Through time, and with constant observation, I noted there were those patients who appeared to have very infrequent fits, also little sign of suffering from any personality problems. I could only assume that in their cases their medication was successfully containing a more normal level of seizure threshold than those having regular fits. If this was so, I was at a loss as to their continued incarceration. Having no opportunity of laying hold of their case-papers, I couldn't come to any firm conclusions about my observations. As regarding the opinion of other staff, I almost found their conjectures on such matters to be biased in favour of the institution. What I had learned through the years appeared to indicate that once an institution got anyone on to its files, it seemed very reluctant to part from them. I had also learned, through my reading, that in the early part of the last century, the keepers who managed the newly-built Public Asylums and Workhouses, had a vested interest in both gaining, and keeping hold of their inmates, and in a lesser degree the subordinate staff also had an interest in keeping a full house. Perhaps such instincts were still operational!

Being cooped up in this institutional environment all winter, the return of spring was a blessing indeed; for unlike their more unfortunate long-term brothers, in the mental hospitals, who got no further than the airing courts, the patients in this colony could look forward to enjoying months of outdoor leisure activities in the evening after work, and all day on weekends. Football, cricket, tennis, sports days; and of course country walks. One could almost feel morale rising at the dawn of spring; tempers were less frayed, and staff and patient relationships took on a more harmonious note. During winter, the long dark evenings meant a return to the constant struggle to sustain morale, especially among the younger men. There is no doubt, as the months increased to years of incarceration, that this extended their difficulties, their nagging thoughts, often expressed, that they may never leave the colony and live a normal life outside. The presence of the older long-term residents, was a reminder to the younger patients of their dim future. It is no wonder that some of them developed personality problems, and were readily prone to agitation requiring constant tact when dealing with them.

The longer I remained in this colony, the more I was at a loss as to why so many people looked upon the epileptic with fear and superstition; their malady apart, they were just like the rest of us, wishing to live a normal life as much as possible!

In no time at all I was being pressurised to become part of the Saturday afternoon staff team, to play against the patients. A pity really, for I had never indulged in any form of sports, nor had I any real interest in such pastimes; as a boy, the only game I had ever played was Cowboys and Indians. However, on the football field I proved I was as fit as the rest of them, but there was no danger of my scoring goals.

In September, Kathy kept reminding me of my promise to move to Bedford. The country walks I had discovered during the months of our stay were so appealing, I wished I was on my own again, and could please myself! However, anything for a quiet life, and so reluctantly I consented.

Two weeks after arriving there, behold Kathy, anxious to have me employed in the same occupation as herself, grandly told me one morning that she had been working the oracle again! An offer to manage a bed-and-breakfast hotel in North London.

St Mary Abbotts

The hotel had once been a private house, a large double fronted building. Every room in the house, apart from the dining room and lounge, had been partitioned to make two rooms. The proprietor spent at least two hours on our arrival lecturing us on the principle of economy; he appeared infatuated with the subject. Our joint wage, which was remarkably small, was enhanced by his providing us with full board, which sounded all right; until we realised that every meal would have to consist of bacon, egg, sausage, tomatoes, bread and cereals! He no doubt expected no one but fools to accept such terms, considering the work was more or less a twenty-four hour post; for he expected the night-bell to be attended to, no matter what the hour.

"We cannot afford to lose custom in this business," said he, addressing me as though I were a new partner, instead of another fool! I had allowed Kathy to travel to London to inspect the layout; she couldn't have been taking much notice of what he had relayed to her.

Ironically it was Kathy, who at the end of the first week of slavery, began to rebel. By the end of the second week, she refused point blank to have anything to do with the work. So she worked the oracle again; and I co-operated solely because in her new post as cook/housekeeper in a private preparatory school in Chelsea, I would be independent and seek my own job; which I found within days. I began work as a Conference Clerk, for the British Institute of Management in Holborn.

Early in January, Kathy became ill with flu. Our accommodation was dependent on Madame having a cook/housekeeper in order to keep her business going. So I packed my job in and took over Kathy's post! Kathy was an excellent cook. Yet within days of my taking over, Madame was openly praising my own cuisine. I didn't mind, but I wished Madame had been a little more tactful; she kept visiting Kathy in her room, and telling her how good she thought I was. As soon as Kathy recovered the flag went up. It was time for our next move.

This time it was to Charterhouse School with myself as cook-in-charge, and Kathy as my assistant. Though I was proving to myself that I could cook, and for large numbers, I thought it a liberty that because I was male, that someone like

Kathy, who was a very good cook, and had years of experience behind her, was on a lower scale than myself.

Kathy bless her, I soon discovered, was scanning the vacancy columns again; she was becoming worse than myself for wishing to be on the move! Little did it dawn upon me that it was her lack of security that was one of the main causes for her always finding fault with whatever work we took on. Myself, I wished I was back on the wards.

She brought to my attention similar posts being advertised for St Bees School, Cumberland. I was acquainted with the area, having tramped round there in the past; the scenery was beautiful, so why not! We were invited up to look around, agreed to the terms, and so accepted the posts.

Three weeks after moving in, we fell out with the management over wages that didn't match with what we thought we had agreed on. So, back to Bedford once more. When I observed Kathy was yet again scanning the Domestic Vacancy Columns, I realised it was time to make another move on my own. On a Saturday morning, after Kathy had gone out shopping, I hurriedly packed my suitcase and left the lodge; I was in no mood for private domestic service.

On my arrival in London, I lodged my case in the luggage office, and immediately began my hunt for accommodation. After spending the weekend in a small hotel, by the Monday I was able to move into a furnished room in Hammersmith. I was busy unpacking my case when I heard a knock at my room door; opening it I was greeted by a thick-set character, about my own age.

"How do! My name is Henry, I'm your next door neighbour; I've just called to ask you whether you'd like a cup of tea?"

"Thanks very much, Henry. Shall I come into your place?" I asked.

"That would be best. What shall I call you, by the way?"

"Tom, is my name. Tom Callaghan," I replied, following him into his room.

The floor was littered with weight-lifting apparatus, though he made no attempt to move any of it, and I stepped carefully over the dumb-bells in order to reach one of the two chairs in the room.

"There's some money's worth there, pal," Henry commented, referring to the numerous pieces of heavy metal equipment. After he had massed the tea in a large teapot, he filled three pint mugs, sweetening and colouring the tea by means of tinned Nestle's milk.

"I'll go over the hallway and give Isaac a call," said he. "We always have our tea together." He soon returned, in the company of a red-faced middle-aged man, dressed in a grey suit and a white silk cravat round his neck. He offered me his hand:

"I'm Isaac. Pleased to meet you, Tom. You're in good company now! Are you a weight-lifter, Tom?" he enquired; chuckling to himself as he did so. On observing that Henry ignored the humorous taunt, I refrained from answering the question.

"What's for tea, then Henry?" asked Isaac.

"Boiled eggs, beetroot and pickled onions," replied he, busy placing six eggs into a pan of boiling water on the gas cooker.

"We like our grub here, Tom" said Isaac. "Tell you what, considering there's three of us, I'll pop into my room, I've got a tin of corned beef."

"Don't count me in," I protested. "The mug of tea will do me fine." But both of them overruled my objections, so I agreed to stay for tea, and Isaac went into his room for the beef, and also another chair. When the meal was over, and the washing up completed; Henry began moving back the tables and chairs to the walls, and opened the window wide. He then stripped to the waist and secured leather support straps on his wrists. I looked on in amazement, before commenting:

"Surely you're not going to do weight-lifting exercises so soon after a meal?" And Isaac, on witnessing the obvious look of incredibility on my face, burst out laughing uncontrollably; but Henry, ignoring him, stooped to grab hold of the massive-looking dumb bells.

"We better move to my place, Tom, and drink our tea in safety," said Isaac, as tears of mirth began rolling down his cheeks. "Once Charles Atlas, here, gets swinging those dumb bells around, no one is safe. He's heading for a hernia, one of these days."

The moment I entered Isaac's room I sensed he must be a long-term tenant; and not a drifter like myself! Three of the four walls were taken up completely with well-stocked bookshelves. His bed corner was screened off by long red satin curtains, and even his gas cooker, and washbasin were concealed by colourful screens.

If Henry's room resembled a scrapyard: Isaac's room, was a haven.

I was immediately drawn towards the bookshelves; each shelf, as I discovered being carefully indexed.

"This library must have cost you a few shillings, Isaac," I ventured. He began chuckling merrily; I sensed he was about to enlighten me about some secret regarding his collection!

"I'll tell you about my library, Tom; but keep it under wraps. You see, Henry works in a hospital, as a porter; and from time to time, visitors bring boxes of books to the gate lodge, for distribution to the wards; but some of the ward sisters won't have anything to do with them; they gather too much dust according to them. So,

Henry takes his pick of the books and gives them to me. Do you like reading, Tom?" he asked.

"It's one of my main pleasures in life" said I; continuing to admire the collection.

"Well then, you're welcome to borrow any time. I've got classical novels by various authors: Russian, French, British, German. I've got philosophy, poetry, politics, astrology and astronomy; take your pick," said he.

"Thanks, I will take up your offer, Isaac. I suppose you do a lot of reading yourself," I suggested.

"Very little. That surprises you, Tom, I'll bet. All I study is astrology and astronomy; you see Tom, and keep this under wraps also, I'm pretty keen on fortunetelling! And I can assure you I'm good at it. According to Rosa, a Hungarian lady, who lives up on the floor above; she claims I'm psychic. She ought to know, she's a Medium!" He winked at me in a serious manner. "She's a very unusual woman. I'll introduce you to her sometime."

He beckoned me over to a chest of drawers and opened the top one, to reveal a crystal ball, black cover-cloth, cards and other fortune-telling paraphernalia.

"What is the idea of the library then, if you read very little?" I enquired.

"Ah!" he uttered significantly. "The sight of all those neat and impressive looking books impress my clients, Tom. Mind you, I'm no charlatan, oh no – not indeed; I can read hands as easily as I read the *Evening Standard*," he insisted confidently.

"I suppose all of your clients are women," I remarked innocently. But my comment did not fool him, he smiled as he replied:

"All of them are, except one elderly shopkeeper; but this only proves that women are more curious, Tom; and not as you're probably assuming, more impressionable. Let me tell you, the majority of women in this world are not fools, at least none of my clients are; they would soon detect anyone coming the old kidology with them. He closed the drawer, then told me to pick a couple of books to read; as I was doing so, he enquired whether I fancied a drink later in some pub.

"How about Henry, shall we ask him?" I asked.

"Henry? He neither drinks nor smokes; he spends most of his spare time developing his muscles. He's not a bad fellow, and kind; but hopeless in conversation," replied Isaac, chuckling good humouredly.

It was Henry, the following morning, who informed me that a gate-porter was required at St Mary Abbotts Hospital, Kensington; he worked at St Stephen's Hospital, Fulham; hence the information. On presenting myself, and after having been interviewed by the Head Porter, then the Hospital Secretary, I was accepted.

There were two gate-porters on each of the three eight-hour shifts: a senior, and an assistant. I began as an assistant; and as the telephonist didn't commence work until 8 a.m., two hours after my own starting time, I had to cope with the hospital switchboard; thankfully the incoming calls at such an early hour were few.

On my second morning, a Thursday, a few minutes after having taken over from the night staff, I was pouring out two mugs of tea, when the sound of an approaching ambulance siren had me rushing outside the lodge to open the gates to enable the ambulance to proceed to Casualty. Fifteen minutes later, it returned, pulling up alongside the lodge, and the crew entered.

"Morning Bill," said the driver greeting my colleague. "Any chance of a cuppa?" he asked.

"Hold your horses, laddie," remarked Old Bill, who was a dry character. "Let's know what you have brought in first," he demanded, picking up his pen and opening the hospital register.

"He's still in the ambulance, matter of fact," replied the driver; "B.I.D. Overdose!" And he began furnishing the details as I poured out tea for both of them. Afterwards, Bill kept an eye on the switchboard, and I accompanied the ambulance crew along the driveway to the mortuary. Once inside it, I entered the details into the mortuary book; then made out an identity tag, to secure to the body of the corpse. I gazed on to the corpse of the young man, who had lived in bedsitter-land; and where, according to the ambulance men, most of the attempted, and the successful overdose victims are discovered in London.

I had no sooner returned to the lodge than Bill, ordered me to go along to Casualty; another ambulance had arrived with a motor-cyclist accident case; I was to assist the general porter in taking the victim to theatre.

After delivering the patient into the hands of the anaesthetist, we donned theatre-dress, then bowled the patient in to the theatre.

"Which one of you is the gate-porter?" enquired the resident surgical registrar.

"I am sir," I replied.

"You have nursing experience, I hear, is that right?" he asked.

"That is right, sir," I replied.

"Good! You stay here, and the other man can go about his other duties," said he. I knew the night porter would inform Bill of the reason for my staying in the theatre.

When the disposable covers were removed from the patient's abdomen, I observed that part of his intestines were protruding; he appeared to be in a right mess! Witnessing the vital parts of the human body being reduced, by means of surgery, or completely removed, was no new experience for me. Therefore I was not really surprised, when in little over an hour, this patient was being neatly stitched up; and the registrar confidently remarking: "He'll do all right!" Both men looked extremely weary, in fact they appeared half-asleep. I learned later, from Bill, that both surgeons had been in bed for less than three hours during the previous twenty-four. Yet they would be expected to continue working the rest of the day, after breakfast time.

"Thank God, I'm only a gate-porter," I remarked to Bill, on being told this. In my opinion, it was a very dangerous practice – to over-work doctors and surgeons, who hold in their hands the lives of sick people.

At 11.30 the same morning, the red-alert phone rang: a cardiac-arrest on one of the female wards. Instantly all other business in the lodge was suspended. In less than four minutes, the duty emergency team, and the porters detailed on this rota to collect the cardiac machine, were all present on that particular ward; saving, we hoped, a life! And Bill was able to record the whole event in the special book kept for that purpose.

It is not surprising to learn that people die in hospital; and in a large metropolitan city, like London, it is to be expected that some of them will not be natives of the place. If any of these individuals were to die in hospital, there are various reasons (apart from pauper funerals), why the next of kin, will decide to have the deceased buried locally, in place of having them transported to their native soil, for their final resting place. I was not long in observing that whenever a relative turned up in such a case, the Mortuary Attendant was usually the first person to be contacted, so as the next of kin could view the body in the Chapel of Rest. This particular gentleman, was not only an efficient operator in the mortuary; he was a good diplomat; very astute when dealing with the bereaved; very anxious to help, very consoling. Relatives would feel so comforted and at ease in his presence; he would have made an excellent undertaker! Before they had left his presence, he would be acquainted with their intentions regarding the funeral. If they had decided against having the deceased taken back to their place of birth, then, if they wished, he would be only to willing to relieve them of all the necessary funeral arrangements!

"Leave it to me. I assure you everything will be done exactly as you wish. I understand how you're feeling, and being in a strange city only makes it more difficult; leave the worry to me." They were only too grateful for the unexpected assistance; and of course they show their appreciation!

"You're very kind indeed," responded he, pocketing the remuneration.

Once they had departed, he asked the switchboard operator to give him an outside line, on hospital business. He always ensured to make such calls from the privacy of the mortuary! He was not that shrewd, he was ignorant of the fact that some telephone operators are as inquisitive as himself. His calls to his favourite undertaker were not as private as he would wish:

"Is that you, Bert? Mack, here. I've got one for you! I'll give you the measurements; and I'll see you when you come for the body!"

There was no doubt he was serving a need; besides expressing his belief in private enterprise.

Being employed in a London general hospital, I was deliberately taking stock of all that was going on around me; not only because I am deeply interested in healthcare, but because I felt I had a personal invested interest; I would like to feel I was in secure hands, if ever I became a patient. Of course I possessed unique opportunities to observe the day-to-day workings of every department. Not only was I engaged in what is really the hospital's vital communications department, but also in a position, at times, to observe the activities of almost every other branch of the hospital: the Casualty department; the wards; the operating theatre; the laboratory; the dispensary; the mortuary and finally the kitchens! The two main drawbacks, in my estimation, were, first, the lack of common sense in the handling and preparation of foodstuffs. I often witnessed cooked meats and desserts left on the kitchen tables, all at the mercy of the flotilla of flies, completely ignored by the night-cook. Underneath the tables, I often observed steeping in water, the vegetables that were intended for next day's lunch!

The second failing, which I was constantly observing, mainly at weekends, was the inhumanly long hours of duty worked by the poorly-paid junior medical staff. From a Friday evening until a Monday morning they were on call, for Casualty, the wards and the operating theatre. It was something to put into their diaries if they ever got one night's complete sleep during that period! I often prayed that if I ever had to be admitted to hospital, let it be during the week and not at the weekend.

I was on my first night-duty shift. It was one a.m., the intercom-phone rang. The maternity ward required the services of the night-porter. He had just left the lodge on one of his hourly patrols round the grounds. As it was quiet at the time, Bill told me to go. When I arrived at the Sister's office, she went into the sluice room, and soon returned with a small bundle in her arms, which she handed over for me to take to the mortuary! On going down in the lift, I thought to myself: What a tragedy; realising that some lonely mother on the ward would be weeping, in place of smiling at her expected new arrival. Returning to the lodge, I collected the keys of the mortuary. As I approached the tree-sheltered building situated in a secluded part of the grounds, I observed a light beaming from the stained-glass window of the mortuary chapel. I assumed someone had left it on accidentally earlier in the evening; I would switch it off before I left. In the mortuary I carefully placed the tiny body on to one of the empty shelves in the cold storage. I was busy writing the necessary details in to the mortuary book, when I detected a slight stir behind me; I turned round and observed that the door handle of the post-mortem room which led through into the chapel was turning. My scalp tingled; I imagined for a moment, that I was about to witness the resurrection of some corpse that had perhaps been overlooked and left on the dissecting table. I was convinced it couldn't be body-snatchers having broken in by way of the chapel room; the days of Burke and Hare were long over and gone forever! I stood my ground, after all I was near the mortuary exit. The door slowly opened, then on the wall I made out the silhouette of a wide-brim trilby and a beard, then wide shoulders: and so came into view, a thick-set, middle-aged Jew! I then realised instantly there must be a Jewish corpse, resting on one of the trolleys in the next room, and that this gentleman must be the 'Watcher' employed by the relatives of the deceased.

I gave out a sigh of relief as I remarked:

"By jove, sir, I thought you were a ghost coming in." He smiled, as he briskly began rubbing his hands; no doubt he was feeling the cold in there.

"Look sir! Me and my colleague are about to make a pot of tea, why don't you come along and have a hot drink; no one's to know you left your post; you're bound to be freezing in there," said I.

"Thanks very much, kind of you, I will accept your offer," he replied. When I entered the lodge, I could sense the lack of surprise registered on the face of my mate, that he had known about the presence of the Watcher, in the mortuary.

"You could have told me, Bill, that there was company along there; I may have suffered a heart attack!" said I.

"That will be the day or night, when you have a heart attack at the prospect of meeting a ghost," remarked Bill, who was busy providing our guest with a mug of tea. Afterwards the Watcher returned to the mortuary.

A few minutes later, we observed through the window, the night-general-porter, in the company of a shabbily-dressed old man who was obviously being lectured at by the porter before being ordered out of the hospital grounds. The porter entered the lodge, muttering indignantly to himself. "Where did that old geezer come from?" enquired Bill, critically.

"He's a tramp I caught kipping alongside the boiler-house," replied the porter, sounding deeply offended at not having caught him on his earlier rounds. "I don't like tramps," he looked appealingly at Bill. "You won't put it down in the report books, will you Bill?"

"Forget it. Have your sandwiches," replied Bill.

"Tramps! I'm sick of them; this bloody city is full of them," muttered George the porter, before he began tackling his huge thick sandwiches, stuffed with dubious-looking potted meat.

"The tramp hasn't put you off your supper," I remarked humourously.

George looked at me cautiously, as though he was expecting me to tap him for one of his unappetising sandwiches, and was about to speak, despite his mouth being full, when the intercom phone rang. Bill answered it. On replacing the receiver, he beckoned to George:

"All right, laddie. They want you on J Ward, to take a treatment card up to Doctor D— in his room."

George rose to his feet in haste to please Bill for not entering the tramp incident in the report book, stuffing half a sandwich in his mouth as he did so.

"Let him finish his supper," Bill, said I, also rising. "I'll do it! Get the card signed and take it back to the ward, yes?"

"That's it Tom. They probably wish to give the patient an injection," he replied.

It was a few minutes after two a.m., as I quietly made my way up the steps to the medical staff quarters. This particular doctor had been busy in Casualty, up to one a.m.

"If I was a forger," thought I, "I would sign the card myself, and let the poor man sleep on, for he had a full day's work ahead of him in the morning! I had got on talking to him one night, and discovered him to be a real down-to-earth character; To pay his way through medical school, he had humped sacks of grain in a mill, been a barman, washed up in hotel kitchens; indeed he had sampled a number of jobs on the casual employment market that I myself had been acquainted with during my time on the road! His room door was unlocked for he always left it so when on call. When I entered, the bed-light was on; he couldn't have been asleep very long, but I had to waken him. He even gave me a tired sort of smile as I apologised for having to disturb him.

One evening we received a major accident alert from the police, at the scene of a nearby tube station. As soon as we had informed the Casualty department, we set about mustering the resident medical staff, and porters, phoning the homes of the consultants, the hospital secretary, and the Head Porter. Everything worked so smoothly, it was a useful lesson, and a tonic; everyone carried on as though such accidents were an everyday occurrence. There had never been any doubt in my mind that Casualty would be able to cope with any emergency; their daily workload gave them all the practice they required to deal with human tragedy of any magnitude.

What the Casualty department was not geared to cope with were the occasional weekend brawling drunks! I remember asking old Bill, on my first night-duty shift, about the cosh which he had brought out of his locker and placed under the desk near the enquiry window.

"You'll probably see why my laddie, before long," he began in his dry fashion. "You might think all the lunatics are in asylums you've worked in; but I can tell you on Friday and Saturday nights here we can get more than our share of madmen!"

As I learned, it was bad enough when only one side of the fracas were brought in to hospital Casualty; but why it was considered necessary to transport both parties of the drunken combat to the same hospital defied all logic and common sense. If all went reasonably well, the hooligans, after having been patched up, showed their appreciation simply by delivering verbal abuse towards the staff as they left the Casualty department; and bid the gate-porters in the same fashion. But unfortunately, there were times when the drunken combatants recommenced fighting each other in Casualty, terrorising the staff and the genuine peaceful patients waiting for treatment. Yet all the assistance they could call upon until the arrival of the police, was one solitary porter; and George, poor fellow, at such times was naturally terrified himself. Usually when they heard the nurse on the intercom-phone urging the lodge to call the police, the pests, though intoxicated, managed to climb over the railings or rushed up the drive towards the gate; it was expedient to open the gate and let them go, for attempting to hold them until the police arrived could result in the lodge being invaded, and perhaps the communication equipment damaged or destroyed.

The most aggravating aspect of such brawling scenes, apart from the possibility of the staff being manhandled, was that one or more of the hooligans may be so badly injured as a result of fighting that they had to be admitted. Then later the Emergency Bed Service might phone in an attempt to have a very sick person admitted, only to be told there were no beds available! Then of course the E.B.S. had to phone around London, desperately trying to find a hospital to accept the case.

Mind you, there is a remedy for this continuous lack of hospital security; especially so in Casualty departments; but the cure is an economic one.

The Seance

One morning, on one of my rest days Isaac invited me into his room for coffee. Elsie, a young lady aged about twenty-two, who came once a week to clean his room out and had her hand read as an extra remuneration, was present. During our conversation Isaac mentioned to me that Rosa was intending to hold a seance that evening; he and Elsie would be there, but another one was required to make up the number of twelve, which was Rosa's ideal party! I agreed willingly to attend.

That evening I entered her apartment in the company of Isaac. She had her own separate bedroom, bathroom and kitchen. All those present in the lounge were standing about gossiping; Isaac and I were the only males. All of the women ceased gossiping when I entered in order to concentrate their attention on to me; each pair of eyes were deadly inquisitive. When I was introduced to Rosa, she fixed her dark, almost hypnotic, eyes upon me and appeared to be attempting to probe my innermost thoughts!

Was I a believer? Or just plain curious?

Elsie arrived; and Rosa excused herself and moved towards Isaac. Elsie was dressed for a party, rather than for a gathering of inquisitive women in quest of Spirit Contact! I made sure I sat next to Elsie; I was convinced that the other women, including Rosa, mildly resented my presence and I thought that if perchance no Spirit turned up during the seance, I would be looked upon as the cause of the absence.

When all were seated, Rosa led a prayer; and apparently I was the only one who was unacquainted with the words of it; the prayer was followed by a hymn; nor did I know the words of this. When this devotional business ended, a table-lamp, situated behind a silk screen was switched on by Isaac, who then switched off the main room lighting. The effect of this was to place Rosa, sitting in her armchair, into shadow. Isaac then requested silence, as Rosa settled down. She began breathing deeply, then it moderated; whether she was in a trance or not, I could not decide from where I was sitting; at least her eyes were closed. For a little while there was continued silence. Then, a sleepy-sounding voice rising from the direction of the armchair, was heard. Instantly the women began peering at each other, and whispering excitedly among themselves, but were quietly rebuked by Isaac. Then the meeting really began in earnest!

"Yes! Yes! I am receiving you," spoke Rosa, in her distinctive foreign accent. "Who are you?…Yes I understand." Having apparently made contact, Rosa began addressing the meeting:

"Does the name Martha, mean anything to anyone present?"

Every one of the women exchanged curious and eager glances with each other; but the response appeared to be negative. I was about to assume that the visiting Spirit, Martha, had turned up at the wrong meeting! But by the determination of Rosa, her mouthpiece, Martha seemed intent on having her visit acknowledged by someone present. And so by insistent and clever deductions, the likes of which would have impressed the great Medium Miss Julia Ames herself, Martha finally managed to ignite a spark of recall in the memory of a dear middle-aged lady sitting on the left-hand side of Elsie. And this lady was becoming more excited by the second. She admitted that Martha had been a very close aunt of her late husband. And when Martha began relating a comforting message from her departed husband the poor lady almost swooned; however, controlling her emotions, she attempted to converse with the dematerialised visitor, as though both of them were using the phone! But a gentle admonishment directed towards this near-neurotic woman by Isaac was the cue, as it turned out, for Martha to suddenly decide her time was up. The seance continued and most of the women present were communicated with by either the Spirit of their departed husbands, or some other Spirit, kindly claiming to communicate on their behalf.

I was disappointed that none of those Spirits had decided to liven the meeting by materialising. When Rosa opened her eyes to indicate that she had fully returned to our presence, Isaac switched on the ceiling-light, and turned off the table-lamp. Then very discreetly, and almost piously, he handed round a brass plate. Some of the women placed pound notes on the tray, Elsie contributed two half-crowns; my offering was the smallest on the tray; I was convinced that Spirits had no earthly use of money.

Everyone, with the exception of Elsie and myself, gathered around Rosa and Isaac; as they did so I whispered to Elsie, inviting her to a drink.

In the saloon bar of a local pub she told me that tonight's seance had been her fourth experience; I also learned that Rosa too told fortunes.

"Do you believe there is life, after death Tom?" she asked.

I pondered over her question, wondering whether she was just being curious or seeking assurance that I was a believer. I decided that whatever her opinions were on such matters, I must be honest in my reply:

"I think you ought to look upon the claims of anyone to be able to communicate with the Dead in the same light-hearted manner as you ought to do with the claims of fortune-tellers…"

"I can vouch for Isaac regarding telling fortunes," she interjected; "he's amazing at reading hands. He has told me things about myself which he couldn't have guessed about."

"Probably details which you have unwittingly volunteered during conversations with him in the past," I replied smiling. "And I suppose you believe in Spiritualism too?"

"Well! There must be something in it Tom when brainy men like Sir Oliver Lodge and Sir Arthur Conan Doyle, believed in it. Their books on the subject are full of facts on the questions of life after death," said she with conviction.

"My word Elsie! You have been studying the subject; both Lodge and Doyle were giants of the Spiritualism Movement," said I, surprised that she appeared to have gone to such trouble on the matter. She broke out giggling, before explaining.

"You must be joking, Tom. Me study! It was Isaac and Rosa who told me all that. I'd never heard of those men beforehand."

"Well I have read the works of both those men on the subject; they didn't convince me. Mind you, I was surprised when I did learn that Oliver Lodge believed in Spiritualism; he was a well-known scientist! As regarding Conan Doyle, I'll wager that Isaac hasn't told you that the same man also believed in Fairies. He even wrote a book about them called *The Coming of the Fairies*! This resulted in him becoming the laughing-stock of Fleet Street."

She began giggling once more. I sensed another of her revelations was forthcoming.

"Now it's your turn, Tom, to laugh at me," said she mockingly. "I must tell you, I too believe in Fairies; always have done since I was a little girl. My mother believes in them as well."

"Have you ever set eyes on any Fairy?" I asked. She shook her head; in a disappointing manner. Then replied in a firm tone:

"I've never set eyes upon a Spirit, before; but this doesn't prevent me from believing that there is Life after Death. It is all to do with faith!"

"Elsie! If there is an existence after death as the Spiritualists claim; do you think it an odd exercise for any Spirit to communicate through the offices of a Medium, solely to warn his wife not to leave the gas-taps on before going to bed at night?" I asked; referring to one of the messages supposedly received that evening, from the Other Side!

She couldn't resist a smile, before replying seriously, "I see nothing trite about a Spirit being concerned about the welfare of a loved one, left behind!"

"I give up, Elsie," I remarked smiling. "By the way, does Henry the weight-lifter believe in Spirits and fortune-telling?" I asked.

"No. He says it's all a lot of nonsense" she replied.

"Does he now? Well it proves he exercises more than his muscles," said I.

Kathleen Arrives

I had just stepped out of the laboratory, after having delivered a small parcel that had been handed in at the gate lodge, when I was accosted by the head porter. "There's a woman at the lodge gates waiting to see you, Tom. She claims to be your wife," said he looking at me speculatively. "A nice bit of stuff too; has she any sisters?" he asked.

"She has one sister; I'll let her know about you, when I next see her," I replied.

Kathy was standing outside the gates, dressed smartly in a red, summer frock. I greeted her warmly. "Would you believe it, I was about to drop you a letter tonight," said I; which was the truth, not that I expected her to believe me, for it was over four months since I had left her. Her frown convinced me she didn't believe.

"Mind you, I've got to congratulate you on your detective work; I don't suppose you have any intention of telling me how you discovered I was working here," I remarked. She responded as usual, with her 'Mona Lisa' smile. Later, I found out she had often used the offices of the Salvation Army Missing Persons Bureau, and once even employed a private detective agency. I was impressed that she thought I was worth the bother.

"I've got lovely accommodation for both of us," she began, getting to the vital business, and ignoring my excuses. "I've started work as a cook/housekeeper for a wealthy couple, who live in Cromwell Road only a few minutes from here. We've got the whole of the basement to ourselves. You will come won't you Tom, please?" In fact I was relieved to hear such news.

"You bet I'll come," I replied eagerly. "The house I'm living in at the moment is full of spooks and fortune-tellers. Look, I finish duty at two o'clock; and I'll come straight to Cromwell Road, so have a meal ready; and afterwards if you can, why not come with me to Hammersmith, and help me to pack. And if you wish, I'll get Isaac my fellow lodger, to read your hand for you; he's very good at it, so he says."

"I want no lunatic telling my fortune, I don't believe in such nonsense," she retorted rather indignantly.

The house owned by Kathy's new employer, was quite a large one. They occupied the whole of the ground floor; and considering there were only two of them, they had ample space. Despite being wealthy, they had the other two floors let to two professional couples. Kathy and I had been in this billet about a month when the tenants on the first floor left after serving notice. As they had been long-term residents, during which time the flat had never been decorated, Kathy's employers decided to have it done. On learning this, and unknown to me, Kathy took it upon herself to praise my painting talents to them. So impressed were they, not forgetting they would have the work done far cheaper by me than by employing the professionals, they wasted no time in consulting me! House decorating, until that time, was one of the few jobs I had never tackled, though I never admitted this: to me it was a challenge, and of course I was thinking of the reasonable fee I would receive! So I set to work on my days off, and evenings, or afternoons, depending on what shift I was on at the hospital.

It was a large flat; four big rooms, kitchen and bathroom. It took me nearly a month to complete the job, and the end result even surprised me, despite the fact that I always took on a task with the self-assurance that not only would I be able to cope with it, but I would do it well! This confidence of mine was the product of an early apprenticeship which had commenced at the age of nine, when I had voluntarily taken on the role of odd-job man, in order to assist my hard-pressed parents to make ends meet, selling newspapers, firewood, tatting for rags, and working at Paddy's Market, a rendezvous of second-hand clothing merchants.

I felt a great satisfaction with my first decorating job; there had been no problems of having to cut corners, and no stinting over materials; unlike those poor souls in Tressell's 'Ragged-Trouser Philanthropists' who were compelled to connive at shabby practices in order to hold on to their ill-paid jobs. Though in one sense, I was treated like any one of Tressell's fictional workmen; I was not asked about what I thought I was worth. I was commended highly for my work, then handed twenty five pounds for a month's work. I made no comment; I knew how easy it was to be shown the front door!

But my reward was not lost on Kathy; from that day onwards, to my dismay, she began scanning the vacancy columns of *The Times*. On my refusing to entertain any further private posts she gave in her notice, and of course I had to follow suit.

Then we moved up to North Finchley. I began work as a Theatre Attendant, at Barnet General Hospital; and Kathy once more found work in a branch of Woolworth's.

Though I was no stranger to the basic routine of operating-theatres, I discovered after only a couple of weeks at Barnet General, that my previous theatre experience had been negligible! Apart from the leucotomy operation I had witnessed during my stay at Bexley, in 1944, and the emergency operation at St Mary Abbots, all other theatre experience had consisted mainly of transporting patients from the wards to the theatres, and back again; in between times, I would probably be around the recovery room, therefore absent during the actual operations. But in my new post, as Theatre Attendant, I was witnessing almost daily, for the first time, a variety of surgical operations: appendectomies; tonsillectomies; adenoids; mastoids; colostomies, and ileostomies; amputations; caesareans; the list seemed endless! Tonsils, kidneys, lengths of intestines, sawn off limbs, and other bits and pieces of the human anatomy being dumped into receivers, prior to being taken away for incineration; or perhaps sent to the laboratory for some test or other; with a view of possible more surgery on a particular patient at a later date! At times, I almost felt I was working in some unique abattoir, where humans in place of animals were being systematically butchered, the main difference being that here the majority of the victims survived the ordeal! It is only after a few months of such work, that one begins to realise the countless maladies that can arise in the human anatomy, apart from accidents, which result in one landing up in the hands of the surgical teams.

On the odd occasion I was posted to another theatre, where orthopaedic surgery took place. One afternoon when I turned up, I was surprised at the diminutive appearance of the surgeon, who was having to work from a kind of platform. He reminded me of the midget German tenor, Joseph Schmidt. He was certainly a man of few words; I could never imagine him breaking out in singing some operatic aria!

With few exceptions, what I was continuing to discover whenever I was employed in a non-nursing capacity, was the snobbishness displayed by the doctors, ward sisters, surgeons, especially consultants, towards ancillary staff! But to be honest, I had found such snobbery in all walks of life, even on building sites, where as a navvy I was looked down upon by most of the tradesmen; my heart goes out to such mortals. The human animal is a quaint species; it would take greater men than Freud to understand him; if that is at all possible.

As regarding understanding myself, I had given up that exploration long ago; apart from realising that I was only content whenever I was in work caring for people; the sick in mind, or in body; or the unfortunates in our society – the homeless. But I loved to wander; I was a restless spirit!

And Kathy! For someone who had never, before I met her, ventured far from her own small locality, it seemed she had become also infected with the wanderlust. Who was I to complain? Unfortunately, her choice of occupations were always in private service; no doubt to ensure that I did not escape for a period.

Christmas 1964. Once again we spent a lovely old-fashioned time of it; in the company of our landlord and his mother. I was content with my work, Kathy appeared to be settled.

Come March, and she gave up her job. In April we left for Cheshire, to begin work as nursing assistants in a Home for the Aged.For the next three years, we served in two homes for the aged, and in two mental institutions, in various parts of the country. The in the spring of 1968, we commenced nursing in yet another home for the aged, in Ware, Hertfordshire. It had been a struggle on my part, to insist that I continue to work in the health service. The previous May, 1967, whilst nursing in a hospital, near Brighton, Kathy had pleaded with me, then began agitating, that we have a break from nursing, and go into private service, where we would have our time off together. So I left my post all right, not to take up the domestic skivvy work that would have been my lot, but instead, I hopped over to Calais, and went tramping around the countryside – as far as Boulogne. Returning after eight days, I assumed I had made my point. So on my applying for the posts at Ware, she resigned herself to the inevitable. At least I thought so then!

Towards the end of September, Kathy brought to my notice a certain vacancy in the columns of her favourite newspaper *The Times*.

Lady M–

A s fate would have it I was not too pleased with my present conditions, so reluctantly I agreed to let her apply. As a result, a couple in their forties came to the Home, on my day off; and the interview took place in my room. During the discussion I sensed the urgency of this lady and gentleman to bring the matter to a successful conclusion. After reading our references, the lady accepted our services, on behalf of her aged mother, who resided at the family home at Wrington, a few miles outside Bristol. Her mother, Lady M—, was the widow of Sir John M—, who I believed had at one time been chairman of W. H. Wills, Bristol. Kathy and I served our notice at the home, then travelled to Bristol, being met at the station by her daughter and the same gentleman, who appeared to be a close friend of hers. They assisted us with our luggage into their car and drove us out of the city to a village called Wrington. As it was the month of October, and past seven o'clock in the evening, it was quite dark as we entered the driveway of the estate – past the unoccupied gate-lodge, and stopping outside the main entrance to the old large mansion. There was not a light to be seen, but what I could make out in the gloom reminded me of the description of the house of the eccentric Miss Havisham in Dickens' *Great Expectations.* The whole of the ground floor of the front of the house appeared to be closed up. As we entered the hallway there were no visible signs of occupation, no sound, no light, until the daughter switched them on. Kathy and I followed our escorts along a silent corridor, then through a door into a room overlooking the rear of the house; and what a room! It was very large and magnificent looking. I later learned that it had often served as the ballroom in earlier days.

"Is that you?" called out an elderly lady from behind a large screen, over near the french window. She was sitting on a settee with a small table beside her. So we were introduced to Lady M—, who was ninety-two, partly deaf, and with failing eyesight. But apart from those defects, she still appeared a stately-looking lady. She bid us to sit down beside her, one on either side. Then addressing Kathy by her full Christian name, she asked her would she assist her daughter in preparing a meal for the five of us? Off the pair of them went and the old lady turned her attention to me:

"Callaghan!" she began in a brisk business-like tone, no Christian name terms for me, though being acquainted with the works of such writers as Wilde and Wodehouse, I felt flattered, for I was sure that people like Lady M— would have addressed their butlers, and perhaps their doctors, and bank managers, by their surnames.

"Callaghan!" she repeated, "My daughter will show you around the grounds in the morning. You should find everything in order; though I believe the glasshouses are in need of repair!"

After supper, the daughter took us round the house. We discovered that with the exception of the large ballroom, and the large kitchen and pantry – also overlooking the rear of the grounds – the rest of the downstairs rooms had their windows shuttered; so had a number of the rooms of the first floor! The grand old lady was undoubtedly living the life of a recluse, apart from the presence of a couple of servants. The previous couple had been gone just over a week, leaving this daughter with the responsibility of having to live at Wrington and look after her mother; hence her eagerness to employ us at once, so as she could return to her own home in Hampshire. After showing us our bedroom, she took us into her mother's. It resembled a curiosity shop: there were brown paper parcels galore, shoe-boxes, larger cardboard boxes, bundles of old newspapers, and clocks and ornaments, all forming a natural screen round the large four-poster bed. The whole mansion appeared as though it was waiting for the removal men: carpets were rolled up and dust covers concealed most of the furniture. Back down on the ground floor, Kathy went into the kitchen and accompanied the daughter down into the cellars to be shown the oil-firing central-heating system, which I would have to keep an eye on daily. "The wine cellars are empty" she remarked, as I made to enter. My hopes of the odd bottle of wine on the house were instantly dashed. On returning upstairs from the basement, she told me that her mother had an account with the village grocer, and butcher; from those two shops we would get all our needs, and her mother would make out their cheques on a Saturday morning each week, along with our pay cheques.

Next morning, after breakfast, the daughter escorted me round the grounds, before she left for Hampshire. At the sight of the neglected gardens, lawns and glasshouses, I wondered on what the gardeners of the past had employed themselves at during their stay, for I could not detect any recent signs of cultivation, not even keeping the grounds tidy. She must have sensed my critical feelings at the way I was looking around me.

"Goodness knows what the last gardener has ever done, apart from eating and sleeping," she remarked!

However, I promised myself that by next spring I would have changed the dismal scene so dramatically that this handsome-looking daughter of Lady M— would begin to wonder whether I was in league with the Little People; or perhaps blessed with supernatural powers! And so she left me and returned to the house. I began meditating, thinking that gardening, like the arts, is an occupation that brings one into close communion with the soul. Along with nursing, which I like, gardening was an employment that so engaged one's whole interest that one would never consider the flight of time! However, two hours later, my stomach reminded me that it was break-time.

Returning to the grounds I set to work once more and loving every minute of it. At twilight, I put my tools away, and sat down on a bench, back to daydreaming! How I would have loved to have been on this estate during its heydays: I could almost picture the various scenes of its many May times: the blossom on the fruit trees and bushes, also on the vines in the glasshouses; the flower gardens beginning to show-off as usual, and the huge kitchen gardens that would have supplied the house, and the staff, with vegetables all the year round. I was convinced I was observing a one-time horticultural paradise that was suffering from at least ten years of sad neglect. In days gone by, there would have been a number of men working in its grounds; now there was only myself; yet I felt great being alone in this private kingdom, with no one to bother me by attempting to impose their own work-plans of rejuvenation; I was beginning to work out in my mind as to how I would bring everything back to life!

After my evening meal, I went to attend to Lady M—; this I was expected to do each evening in order to tell her what I had been working at in the grounds. It was obvious to me that no one had informed the old lady what state the grounds were really in, and I saw no reason to shatter her illusions. She had me to sit on the sofa next to her, which saved me from raising my voice. No sooner had I completed my report than she dismissed me. Leaving her, I walked along the corridor and entered the library of her late husband, which was some distance from the ballroom. The windows being shuttered made it all the more cosy on such wintry nights! The library, to me, was like entering a literary Aladdin's Cave; shelves of books from floor to ceiling, and what a selection: poetry, politics, religion, history, biography, the classics, fiction, and most of the authors I was already getting acquainted with; though here were some of the novels I had yearned to lay my eyes on; all I ever wished to read was here under one roof; at last I had my own study and library. I felt spiritually at home! Thankfully, television was available for Kathy, for goodness knows what she would have done to amuse herself in such a large rambling house that appeared, internally at least, as though prepared for a siege.

The kitchen was also a huge place, one end of it taken up with the flat-topped stove, now generated by oil in place of wood and coal. The views from its windows were magnificent, in the distance could be seen the Mendip Hills. One early evening, sitting on one of the kitchen benches having a cup of tea and peering out of the windows, I was suddenly rewarded by the vision of one of the loveliest and exciting sunsets I had ever seen in my life; that one glorious picture alone was worth the trouble of coming back to Somerset, for I had tramped round the country many years beforehand.

One evening, on my regular calls to discuss the day's work in the grounds, Lady M— appeared to be in a talkative mood; after completing the day's business, she began showing me through her two photo albums: scenes of the 1920s and 30s. Pictures of her husband and herself, her two daughters and son: shots taken of tennis matches in progress; parties on the lawns; a ball in progress; I was fascinated by the dress of some of the ladies in the ballroom, including herself – appearing as a smart-looking woman.

There was no doubt the old lady was enjoying escorting me down memory lane, and in me she had an avid listener. Thereafter on an evening she would continue reminiscing about her bygone days. Though at times she appeared to forget what she had related to me two days previously, she proved to be able to recall scenes and incidents of her youth so vividly that I felt almost transported back into time – along with her. Her talk belied her great age; and she impressed upon me how proud she was of her social background; no condescending humbug with her; I learned more from her conversation on how the minds of people in her social class worked, that I could have gained by reading those foolish romantic novels that were full of fancy tales of ladies from wealthy families eloping with penniless wanderers like myself! Mind you, I believed her when she stated she was in love when she married her late husband; though it would be no coincidence that both of their families were well to do. She convinced me by her talk that she would never have married anyone outside her class. If perchance I had been around at the time, and crossed her path, my poverty would have ruled out any chance of gaining her hand in marriage, despite my possessing a fine tenor voice! As a matter of fact I did sing to her one evening and earned her praise.

One of the problems of numerous individuals who are wealthy, and attain great age, is that they begin to assume that if they are not careful in money matters, they might end up a pauper! Every Saturday morning was the time of reckoning: I would attend Lady M—, and patiently coax her to sign our pay cheque, meanwhile she would be attempting to put off the issue until the following morning, or until the Monday. When the tradesmen's accounts were due to be paid, the same tortuous procedure would have to be gone through in order to get her to sign their cheques. The poor soul was living in the past and could not grasp why things were so expensive. Indeed if I had taken notice of her, Kathy and I, and herself, would have existed solely on bread and vegetables. But after I had phoned her elder daughter in Hampshire, I was told to order from the tradesmen what was necessary, within reason. The old lady was wealthy, yet wouldn't believe it! Kathy and I didn't need reminding we were poor; and with the wages we earned, no matter where we worked, we were destined to remain in that mean state forever more.

One morning as I was working in the grounds, Kathy came out to me and remarked that Lady M— wished to speak to me. I entered the ballroom silently; though she was hard of hearing and having poor sight, she sensed as always my presence:

"Is that you, Callaghan?" she called out in her usual commanding tone; "I know you're there," she said almost challengingly, having given me no time to respond.

"Yes, it is me, Lady M—. I'm busy in the garden at this time of the morning," said I, not wishing to be held up. But she insisted I sit down on the sofa in my usual place, then informed me that her younger daughter and her husband were arriving that afternoon and would be staying overnight. I also learned, her husband was a cousin of Lord Home.

"Your wife shall be preparing a dinner for tonight," she continued, directing me to go out to the butcher, and the grocer, and the wine merchant! For this occasion, at least, economy was to be ignored; until later, when she learned it had to be paid for.

"Now I had better give you the money for the wine, because I don't have an account with the wine merchant any longer," and she began exploring into her handbag.

That evening after dinner, her son-in-law, came into the kitchen to talk to us. I was amazed at the similarity between him and Lord Home; they could have been taken for twins. He was a pleasant man to talk to; and of course I talked about Lord Home, and his brother, the playwright.

That night of course I had to forsake my usual abode in the library; instead I sat in the fine old warm kitchen with Kathy, and we too sipped our wine.

With the running of an estate; a unique library at my disposal in the evenings, and winter appearing more like spring, I was prepared to remain in this lucky valley for the rest of Lady M—'s days on earth; and as old as she was I hoped she would last another twenty years! But alas, I wasn't aware that Kathy was once more scanning the vacancy columns of *The Times.*

One day on entering the kitchen to have lunch, Kathy, holding up a copy of T*he Times,* and looking eager, told me that she had just got her eyes on a wonderful job, in London! "It's for a Cook/Housekeeper; and the husband to follow his own occupation. How about it dear? I've had enough of this hibernation."

"I happen to like the job here, and after all, you talked me into it," said I. "Let us stay here – at least until the spring," I suggested.

"But we get no time off. We were promised the son would come to relieve us every two weeks; he only lives a few miles away," she complained.

"Take my word, he won't come sitting around all day; that is why these people employ servants. But then you were aware of the conditions before we came here. So I'm staying," I replied.

She began massaging her hands in a display of silent fury, then raised her voice suddenly: "Then I will leave on my own"; she retorted angrily. I ignored her; convinced she would never do it. A few days later, after breakfast, she remarked, much to my surprise:

"I'm leaving, either with you, or on my own. My bags are already packed."

"I can't look after Lady M— on my own; show her to bed and so on," said I, almost speechless with annoyance. "All right, you win this time girl. But no more private jobs in the future," said I, feeling frustrated.

I phoned up the son and told him to come and take over!

The Geriatric Hospital

After a short stay in Bristol, we returned to London in March, 1969. Kathy found employment as an assistant cook, in a Jewish Home for the Elderly; accommodation being provided for both of us. Within two days of moving in, I had found work as a Nursing Attendant in a geriatric hospital, in the same district.

This hospital at Tower Hamlets had once been a workhouse; and like most such institutions, had been built to appear soulless, forbidding and uninviting. Unfortunately for those having to spend their last days on earth inside it, the interior appeared little better. I could well imagine within a short period of having to enter into such an environment as a patient, all hope being abandoned.

This would not be my first experience of nursing in a geriatric hospital, so I was prepared for the unavoidable early morning bustle as I entered on to the ward; for though I realised the night-staff would have begun their usual routine at 5.30 a.m. or earlier, there is far too much to be done – with the small staff numbers on duty. Securing an apron over my white coat, I began assisting one of the patients off a commode; as I did so I observed in dismay his sore-looking buttocks, goodness knows how long he had been sitting on the pot. I put on some zinc ointment, hoping to ease the poor fellow; I was fully aware that the patients would have had their backs rubbed by the night-staff; but I had always been of the opinion that it would have been far wiser to attend to them after they had used the commode, or bedpan, considering the poor souls were often left on them for ages. I put another two patients back to bed, and towed others from bed to armchairs. As I worked, I promised myself to get to know the full names of each patient in turn, as was my usual custom, to avoid addressing each individual as Mister! I didn't think many of them were too keen to be addressed in such an indifferent manner; I was only too well aware that in such places, they were apt to be denied far too much personal identity, privacy and dignity.

By the time I had washed out the commodes and sputum mugs, breakfast had arrived on the ward. Those able to feed themselves were served first, then we, the staff, began to feed those patients unable to cope themselves. As I fed my patient,

I glanced round the ward at the other staff who were similarly occupied; I was not in the least surprised at the feeding methods of one particular Attendant, who would have made a fair ship's stoker: he was spooning into the patient's mouth, barely allowing him time to swallow the previous mouthful, let alone chew his food. Finally, I observed this particular patient wave aside such ridiculous treatment; obviously willing to deny himself rather than put up with such mismanagement! In the past, in the mental hospitals, I had often witnessed some individual nurse who appeared to have little tolerance when it came to feeding handicapped patients. But in a geriatric hospital, the inmates were not certified, and so would often deny themselves when faced with such unsympathetic feeding methods. Yet, I felt sure that if such attendants were to be given the task of feeding an infant, they would have done so with patience, even pleasure. But towards old and infirm people, they appeared to lack understanding and sympathy.

After breakfast, and having completed the bottle-round, we began a bathing session. Not unlike some children, there are old folks who if it was left to their own choice would never agree to be submerged into a bath of water; they will make any excuse in order to avoid having a bath; and if they are able to, even resist it. Under such circumstances one can be excused for resorting to bribery; perhaps a cup of coffee afterwards, or a smoke, or some sweets; certainly the employment of tact and the possession of a good sense of humour are paramount. My own particular method in dealing with such resistance was to begin preparing the bath, meanwhile singing songs which I was certain they would know, and encourage whoever I was intending to bathe to join in, and it always seemed to work. Of course most of my successes in this direction had been in institutions where the patients were mobile, and thus I would be working single-handed. But in a geriatric hospital, and due to the regular infirmity of the patients, it required two attendants to lift in and out of the bath. And of course, if one's partner did not appreciate the method of song, or other tactful means of coaxing the water-shy patients, then the task was not always a smooth one.

By 11.30, the bathing was over for the morning. My next task before the lunch-trolley arrived, was to change the colostomy bag of a particular patient. Unfortunately, he was also suffering from the after-effects of a stroke, and as yet had not regained his speech. When I placed the screens around his bed, he gazed up at me in anxiety as if pondering what kind of attendant I may be. I smiled at him in a reassuring manner, and began talking to him as I set to work; I was aware from past experience, that anyone recovering from a stroke which had impaired their speech, still desired to be conversed with, and not ignored, as though they were devoid of sense and feeling. And his responses told me that he was quite following my remarks, and pleased with them. After lunch, another bottle round, then the Charge Nurse came up to me and enquired how I was making out. He appeared to be an intelligent and compassionate man; and I was pleased to hear him remark that he thought of his patients in the same kindly way as he would his own father.

"We all have to face old age if we live long enough, Mr Callaghan, and I would like to think that when my turn comes, I will be treated with kindness and respect," said he.

I chanced his displeasure by remarking, "Mind you, I wouldn't like to end my last days in one of these places."

"God forbid," he replied; as he began directing me round the ward introducing me to every patient in turn. Another important factor I observed in his favour was that he included in the conversation every patient whose bed we stood over; he did not talk over their heads as though they were absent. It was a most dignified way of dealing with individuals who are often ignored as having no feelings whatever. Too often I had witnessed doctors, and Charge Nurses, standing over the bed of a particular patient, discussing his case-history as though he was blind and deaf to their presence. I don't suppose offence is intended, but a little more thought to the person in the bed listening with dismay, would be appreciated.

When my shift was over, I was grateful to be able to leave behind the dismal scene and get out into the fresh air. From 7 a.m. we had been on the move continuously, apart from a mid-morning break, working like glorified navvies. Yet, as I walked out the gate, the usual feeling of satisfaction which I always felt when engaged in caring for all those who have always belonged to the most vulnerable section of our society, could never leave me; for sure it wasn't the wages that kept drawing me back to such work!

It was visiting time! Those precious moments, that appear to restore to life the most despairing inmate, for without such visits there would only be meal-times to look forward to. A relative or friend, who for an hour or so will attempt to divert them from the dull, and often pointless hospital routine, and sometimes indifference they are subjected to. Someone who has the time to talk to them as an individual and not a bed-number in an institution. Someone who will listen to their complaints, whether rational, exaggerated, or imagined, and hopefully be able to assess which, and so reassure them.

Those who never seemed to have visitors had only their own mental resources to rely on. Fortunately at such times as visiting, most of the usual ward-routine was suspended, thus some of us used the opportunity provided to encourage these lonely men to talk or to reminisce. Some of them, once they began to delve into their memory closet, produced results which were usually not only interesting, but of real social value. Out of their lockers they would bring photos, and newspaper-cuttings of the past, all of which assisted them in their recollections. This is why, through all the years I had been employed in various institutions, I had made it my business to talk with any inmate who was capable of responding, the rewards of which were an education I would have regretted missing.

The main barrier for staff who would spend more time in communicating with lonely patients is the workload entailed in a geriatric hospital; there is so much to do and so few staff to do it; most of the patients are in need of constant attention if they are to be kept reasonably comfortable. Unfortunately the inescapable routine appears to be: feed them, keep them clean, attend to their normal bodily functions, give them medicine; and talk down to them.

One thing in my work which I always resented, was to witness an attendant scolding a patient for having wet the bed! Chiding any bed-wetter, be it a child, or an old person, instead of attempting to seek the cause of their problem, was only another thoughtless display of ignorance. For an old person especially, signs of incontinence, are the ultimate indignity, without having to be rebuked in front of a ward full of strangers! I believe attendants who behaved in that manner, had drifted into such employment simply because it was a steady job. It is no wonder that old folks who are admitted into such places often begin to accept they are a burden. If they are able to be out of bed during the day, then they had better learn to sit still in their armchairs and not move about getting in the way of the staff. If one appears over-active, probably through boredom, usually diagnosed as being confused, they could end up being secured in their armchairs by means of bedsheets; or given tranquilisers! In one institution I nursed in, elderly patients who were in the habit of getting out of bed at night to visit the toilet, instead of asking for a bottle, were secured in bed by the same bedsheet method. This of course can be terrifying for anyone who does not see anything wrong in what to them is a natural and more hygienic habit than the use of bed utensils!

But then, in twenty-five years during which I had worked in almost every type of institution that was organised for the care of the physically and mentally handicapped, I had come to the firm conclusion that the whole set up was lacking in imagination. A great pity really, for with sufficient funding, an imaginative administration, and sufficient, well-trained caring staff, the stigma of the institution could be abolished; and in its place we could create an atmosphere of a well-run guest house, with perhaps a couple of cats around, reminding the guests as much as possible of home. But as things stand, the Powers-That-Be seek to resolve social commitment towards the poor and impotent by ignoring them whenever possible, or by incarcerating them in under-funded overcrowded institutions, where they are sometimes treated with indifference.

Meanwhile on the domestic front, I was aware that Kathy was having problems in the kitchen! It appeared that Orthodox Jewish cookery was beyond her patience; having to keep separate pans for various dishes was to her all nonsense. I wondered really whether it was the usual clash of personalities. She never did appear to work in harmony for too long with members of her own sex. One afternoon on returning from work I discovered she was out; as it was her day off, I thought nothing of her absence. She returned shortly after four o'clock. I sensed she had something to tell me. She suggested a walk after tea. I knew then, we were heading for another move.

It was a lovely evening so we walked up to Whitechapel and then continued down into Fleet Street, and called in to the Old George Inn.

"I've an idea what you have to tell me," said I, "but I assure you I'm remaining at my present job. Well let me hear what you have to say." She began rubbing her hands in agitation.

"I can't get on with my job in the kitchen, it's too complicated – We have to be out of our flat by Friday evening, so there. I can't help it." The beer was in excellent condition and I was enjoying it; thank heaven something was all right.

"Have you found other accommodation then?" I enquired.

"We move into Lady Arthur's house, on Friday evening, in Kensington," she replied, looking at me anxiously. "I'm her new cook/housekeeper," she added. I realised it was going to be quite a journey to get to my job, especially on early shift.

"You know what?" I began feigning dismay, "You're becoming far worse than I am when it comes to flitting from job to job. However, I suppose I'm to blame, you did have a good work track record when I first met you. But remember, I'm staying at the hospital."

She didn't appear concerned at my resolve; after all she was taking up another post, where she could keep an eye on me and ensure I didn't do a midnight flit; she would find some place in the house at Kensington where she could place the suitcases out of my reach, until the day we both moved out. She would have made a good prison wardress.

Kathy had for some time been complaining to me about being on her own in the basement flat whenever I was on night duty, now that the nights were drawing in. On considering her fears, I agreed I would look around for another post, a daytime job.

Cook's Progress

Towards the end of October, I succeeded in gaining the post of Chef, at the Red Cross hospital for Retired Officers, at Putney. There had been doubts expressed by the Matron as to the distance I would have to travel if I were appointed! I soon proved it was no problem to arrive at the Home, from Kensington, on week-days by six-thirty on a morning. Though on Sundays due to lack of early public transport, I was compelled to leave my billet at four a.m., and walk down into Fulham and over Putney bridge, up the hill, then over Putney Common; a walk guaranteed to sharpen anyone's appetite for breakfast; and a trek that probably only a fit ex-hobo would consider!

This was my fourth position in charge of my own kitchen, which was real progress, considering I had gained experience at cooking solely by the means of observation during my washing-up days when I was a tramp. In my first kitchen, and unobserved, I relied on that past experience, plus my cookery book concealed inside my jacket.

From day one at Putney, I was soon in my stride and enjoying my work; though I was puzzled as to why my second-in-command, a lady, who had been employed in the kitchen for quite some time before my arrival, had not been placed in charge, and a second cook advertised for. The world is full of injustices.

Though the menus in this establishment were more varied than those of the public schools I had worked in, nonetheless the diet was still plain, in comparison to the menus prepared in the large London hotels I had also worked in!

I never discovered what battles any of these ex-military gentlemen had fought in, but by all accounts it seemed they must have never been too far, or too long away from an Officers' Messroom. Naturally my working in the kitchen prevented me from having much discourse with any of the residents, though any conversation I did have with them appeared to concentrate on food; the preparation and the cooking of it. They had points to make, and I was only too pleased to listen. On one particular dish, meat, especially roasts, I earned their praise from the beginning, for not overcooking the joints. They also made suggestions as to what kind of cakes and pastries I ought to make for afternoon tea, and I responded willingly. I only wished the inmates of all the other institutions I had worked in, could have had the same opportunity to voice their likes and dislikes to the cooks.

In a busy kitchen, cooking for numbers, there are few idle moments; but in the preparations for Christmas, time is at a premium; more than ever team-work is essential, not only among the various cooks, but including those working in the scullery! From the beginning of my cook days, I had practised the principle that a contented kitchen and scullery staff made for a happy work-place, and in the first instance I ensured that the appetites of the staff were well catered for. Regarding preparing for Christmas, I was determined I was going to make the Christmas puddings, my first ever; it would be my crowning glory as a cook, as I was already pretty adept at the usual culinary dishes; so I resisted all attempts to be relieved of the special chore.

When that day arrived, my first Christmas in my own kitchen, I entered the dining room with the large Christmas pudding and set it down in the middle of the table, poured a noggin of brandy of it then ignited the spirit! I stood back, observing the throng of merry faces, their eyes all lit up, appearing every bit excited as children, and listened to all the congratulations, from the Matron, a fine Irish lady; the Committee Chairman, and all those at table! Charles Dickens himself, would have enjoyed the scene. And I could not but help thinking at that precise moment. If only all those road-travellers who had known me in the past, when I had simply been scrubbing pots and pans, and kitchen floors, during my menial days, could have witnessed my present success, I would have been hailed by all of them as King of the Tramp Majors!

Mind you, though I had proven to myself that I was able to take-up where I had left off since my last position as cook-in-charge, I never for one moment fooled myself. I realised that in all four establishments where I was cook-in-charge, all that was required of the catering staff was good plain cooking; and economics was one of the major reasons why this was so. Therefore it was my opinion that those who are employed in such places never gain the wide experience of the top chefs who are employed in the London Savoy, or any top catering houses in the capital, or elsewhere. I accepted my limitations in that sense.

So New Year 1970 arrived. I was content for the moment, and looking forward to remaining at work in the kitchen, at least until the arrival of spring, when I intended, hopefully, to return to the hospital wards!

Gardener to a Whiz Kid

E arly in March, Kathy told me she was fed up with working as a housekeeper for Lady Arthur. I suggested she look for a furnished room then we could move out of the tied accommodation, and I would remain at my present job. But she was having none of that!

"No, definitely not. Once we get into a room together, you might decide to do one of your vanishing tricks whilst I was out at work. Our present reunion has lasted quite a while; I don't intend pushing my luck, dear," said she firmly.

Early one evening, on returning from work, I observed Kathy scanning the vacancy columns of her favourite newspaper:

"Look Tom, I've been working the oracle again. Listen to this: 'Cook/house-keeper, and Gardener/handyman; contact by phone only'". I glanced at the details; then poured out a cup of tea.

"I presume you have already phoned the number!" I ventured.

She looked at me appealingly, then brought out my dinner from the oven, before replying:

"We've got an appointment for seven o'clock; with a gentleman called John B— You will come with me, won't you?"

"I may as well, otherwise I'll get no peace tonight. We can have a drink on our way back," I replied.

We made our way to Mayfair. Mr B— interviewed us in his luxurious penthouse flat situated above the offices of his firm. He was a young, tall, slim-built, vigorous looking man, handsome too. He told us, after we had furnished him with all necessary details about ourselves, he required a couple, to look after his home in Brighton.

By the end of the following week we were resident on his small estate, situated not far from Brighton's football ground. It was a fairly large house, over a hundred years old, and not without character in appearance; the servants' flat adjoined one gable-end of the house. As far as private service went, I soon discovered it to be the best number we had come across up to that time; even better than at Lady M—'s, in the sense that Kathy had no housebound person to look after. With our employer being away up in London from Monday to Friday, we could take at least a free afternoon and evening, once a week, so long as we saw to the comfort and welfare of his dog during our absence. It was a Great Dane, a very friendly creature, and I came to like it! Later on during my employment, it accidentally knocked me off my feet, and aggravated an existing back disability of mine. The poor dog was as sorry as myself for the incident; it came and licked my face as I lay momentarily shocked.

Everyone has their idea of what they wish for in a garden, and the larger it is, the more scope one has to shape it to their own personal taste. Most people appear to prefer to have their garden, or estate, looking as though it was the work of a landscape artist. But there are some, and John B— was one such person, who prefer a more natural effect. The gardens at the rear of the house possessed rockeries, terraces, trees, herbaceous borders, and mass clumps of seasonal flowers; and as one climbed the steps between the terraces, one had the impression of being out in the countryside – it appeared so natural; certainly it appealed to the smaller breeds of wildlife, and various flocks of birds. As his magnolia tree was in full bloom, it was a magnificent sight; so much so that even the birds seemed to respect there was something special about it, and in the main, considered it to be out of bounds during flowering time!

One night our boss was the subject of debate on a financial programme on television. I found it most interesting to watch and listen to him, because it gave me an insight to his business side of life, apart from my following his fortunes through the press! After the Second World War, came the property boom. Men like Harry Hyams, Joe Levey, Jack Cotton, Charles Clore, and others, made huge fortunes out of commercial property speculation. In the late Sixties another breed of adventurous financial predator came into being: men who were soon to be labelled the 'Whiz kids', 'High-flyers' and 'Wheeler-dealers'. Many of these young men were well-trained accountancy cadets from the money-making school of financier, Jim Slater. These men manipulated finance rather than property or commodities; they took over industries and companies, mainly to strip them of all their available assets: hence the term 'asset-strippers' being levelled at many of these wizard merchants. One of those men was my boss, John B—. Before he had entered the 'money game', he emigrated to Australia, feeling loathful towards the City, and all it stood for. On his way back from there, overland, he claimed he nearly decided to throw in his lot with the Asian communists. Well if he had done so, I reckoned he would still have made his fortune somehow!

Like most people in positions of power; whether in the game of politics, or in high finance, Mr B— appeared to be able to get along remarkably well with very little sleep. There were times during his weekend visits when I would be making a final patrol around the grounds with the dog, before retiring for the night, when I would observe his form silhouetted against the window of his upstairs study, busy at his desk, probably scheming his current, or the next take-over bid. Yet, if it happened to be on a Sunday night, he would be still on his way next morning by 4.30, or soon after, either en route to his offices in London, or to the airport, for a business trip abroad. It was Kathy who always enlightened me on what time he left, for with her being a light sleeper, she always heard his car going down the driveway.

Kathy appeared to be content with her work; then of course I had discovered at an early date, she was always happier working for a male employer; so within months of being in Brighton, we were almost in a set routine: do our work, take the dog for a walk in the park, and sometimes the two of us would spend the odd afternoon in town. On one such afternoon we were probing around the bric-a-brac stalls, when suddenly I was accosted by two shabbily-dressed men whom I failed to recognise immediately; and to judge by the look on Kathy's face, she was hoping I would disown any former association with the two down-at-heel characters:

"Hellow Geordie – By God, you look to be on top of the world," remarked one of them. Peering at him for a moment, I suddenly remembered where I had met the two of them; it was in a hostel in London, where I had stayed a few days on my return from Dublin, after my abortive attempt to earn a living by practicing chiropody.

"Hellow Mick. And you too, Spud!" I shook their hands warmly. "I see you're both back in your favourite holiday resort," I added.

"You're not selling Old Moore's Almanacks now, I'll wager," said Mick after favourably scrutinising my garb.

"No fear, Mick. Me and my wife, are working in Brighton," I replied, and introduced Kathy to them, who condescendingly shook their hands. "How about coming for a mug of tea," said I; instantly leading the way to a nearby café.

Whilst Mick and I kept up the talk, Spud was amusing himself with a greasy-looking pack of playing cards. He turned to Kathy, and asked her to pick out a card from the pack, and he would show her a trick. But Mick intervened: "Why don't you indulge in conversations, in place of always wanting to occupy your mind with playing cards, and other triviality," remarked he scornfully.

"What can I talk about then?" asked Spud, inquiringly.

"About anything man. You ought to think more often; surely you're capable of doing that … Just examine the way you spend your time! You play with cards, you fiddle about with matchsticks, and conjure up daft tricks that would only amuse a school kid." He looked at Kathy and addressed her: "My mate here kids himself he can look into the future by means of the cards. I don't know why, 'cause like meself, he has no future." He cast his attention once more on to his mate: "Why don't you cultivate the mind that God has given you; pass life away by conversing on serious matters; like Geordie and meself do."

I smiled at the intended compliment; I sensed he was after soft-soaping me. Spud, I observed, appeared a little dejected after all the criticism.

"I keep telling you Michael, I'm no thinker. I got no education when I was a lad; nothin' but strict discipline from me father, an' religion rammed down me throat by me teachers," remarked he.

"If you were taught religion in the right fashion then surely that's all the education a body wants in this world," began Mick. "Don't forget, all the great men of the past were religious minded: there was Julius Caesar, Alexander the Great, Oliver Cromwell, Napoleon, the Duke of Wellington and Hitler; to name but a few.

"You've missed out yourself Mick," quipped Spud grinning mischievously.

"That was deliberate, Spud, for I knew you would do it for me," responded Mick. Spud appeared despondent again.

"I wonder whether there will be a band playing in the park today?" enquired he of Mick.

"Who on earth wants to listen to a band, when they're hungry, and gasping for a smoke," replied Mick, critically. "The clique who attend those band-sessions, are the lonely and the over-dressed and over-sexed widows. The type of women you're searching for, Spud; only they prefer the young strapping military bandsmen. So forget about bands, play with your cards if you get bored."

I could sense Kathy was wishing to leave. So going up to the counter I ordered a further two mugs of tea and a couple of cheese-cobs, and paid for them; as I left I slipped a pound note over to Mick, to share between them. Once outside, I got the rebuke I was expecting from Kathy: "I wish you would stop talking to tramps when I'm with you," she remarked in annoyance. "You really puzzle me, you get to talking to any odd characters you come across. Anyway, why don't the likes of them work for a living?"

"My dear, let me tell you something. At a rough estimate, there are about 100,000 homeless men existing on the streets in this country; least that is the figure I've seen quoted from various sources; and at the present time, there are thousands of conventional citizens signing on the dole and available for work. Therefore does it not prove to you, that men like Mick and Spud are surplus to the economic requirements of the labour market. Another thing, as I've told you before, if it wasn't for men like Mick and Spud, who, whenever they get the opportunity, work as skivvies in hotel and restaurant kitchens, for very low pay, the catering industry would really have to change its ways; for no sensible conventional man or woman would scrub pots and pans, swill bins, and floors for the shocking hand-outs, they describe as wages. I know, I've experienced it all. You're aware that I was once a tramp; I'm not ashamed of that fact. So the next time I come across a homeless man, or men, that I have been acquainted with in the past, just walk away, time I have a few words; I won't be annoyed! Come on dear, let us get back to our mansion and have afternoon tea; we'll talk about millionaires, and to hell with tramps. Let officialdom and society in general deal with the vagrants in their usual manner: humbugging and lecturing to them; anything rather than seriously attempting to eradicate what is really an acute social disease.

One morning Kathy had a phone call from an anonymous ex-employee of Mr B—, apparently a victim of one of his recent take-overs; and he threatened to 'get' Mr B—! Further calls came during the day; and of course she kept our boss informed: who was as usual on a weekday up in London. Mr B— certainly took the threats serious enough to engage the services of Securicor; and as he came down to Brighton that weekend, we had the security men patrolling the grounds until he left on the Monday morning!

At the same time, some of the Labour Members of Parliament, were not being too complimentary towards him: 'Asset-Stripper' being one of the milder criticisms! The remarkable thing about such men, who play the 'market', and remove numbers of workers from their payrolls and on to unemployment registers, is that they appear to be annoyed, even hurt, at such criticisms of their behaviour.

I had only one good conversation with my boss during my term of employment for him, during which he commented on his business life; he told me that his own position was as safe as gilt-edged securities! But as it was to turn out later on, he was himself to become a victim of the 'take-over merchants' – though his redundancy terms were golden in every sense of the word, even keeping his pent-house flat.

Eighteen months we remained in residence in Brighton; a remarkable record. We then moved on up to Nottingham, in 1972. In 1974, still being in Nottingham, I once again did a flit, whilst Kathy was out shopping! As with all my previous escapes, I assumed I would return to the fold eventually; and no doubt settle down to make a permanent home for both of us; and Kathy certainly deserved this. But I kept putting off my return, telling myself I was not ready for settling down; and of course the years rolled on.

Since 1980, I have made periodic visits to Bedfordshire, hoping I would come across her in the most likely places, if only to be given the opportunity to apologise; but my searches were in vain. I'm the loser; for she had been a good wife to me.

My Jack London Pilgrimage

When I returned home to Newcastle in 1975, I had no idea I would remain there and seek permanent accommodation. Naturally I often became restless, so periodically I took to the road for short periods, usually making my way to my favourite haunts in the Lake District – though always in springtime and summer; my winter treks were over for good.

One afternoon in March, 1984, I had a surprise visit from a stranger, an American! He had been given my address from a local freelance journalist, called Peter Mortimer. Peter, incidentally, had reviewed my book, *Tramp's Chronicle* for *Arts North* the previous year! My visitor was fairly tall, sported a beard and possessed keen but smiling eyes, and was in his thirties – a colourful-looking character, resembling Erroll Flynn's portrayal of Robin Hood.

Over a mug of tea, I learned that he hailed from Oakland, California, the home town of one of my favourite authors, Jack London! My visitor, Stuart Kandell, had his own Theatre Drama Group, based in Berkeley, not far from Oakland. At this time, he was a member of the Newcastle University Group, who were teaching school drama at my old school, South Benwell. Having read my book, *Tramp's Chronicle*, he wished me to join the group for a whole term, and by the means of drama, show the pupils what conditions a tramp could have expected to experience in the 'Spike' on applying for a night's shelter! Of course I agreed; to be an actor had been one of my ambitions when I was a lad; and I fully realised the children would love the game, for all kids are very versatile and possess natural talents for acting.

I thoroughly enjoyed every day of that term, so did everyone else. Away from the school, I got to know Stuart Kandell, and his friend, Karl, from Australia, very well, and the three of us made numerous excursions into the Northumbrian countryside; in the evenings we discussed drama, my contribution usually being on the subject of Jack London, and why so many of the tramps I had met on the road were fascinated by this American writer of 'He-Man' literature. Come the end of their stay, Stuart and Karl returned to their respective countries, both promising to correspond with me.

In June, the following year, 1985, to my amazement, I received an invitation from Stuart Kandell, to visit Oakland, and give some talks on Jack London; and on my own life, and writing! I couldn't put pen to paper quick enough to accept what would be for me my Jack London Pilgrimage!

When I was a boy, during the late 1920s and 1930s, on many a winters night sitting round the fireplace with my brothers and sisters, my father would entertain us with storytelling; some of the stories he would make up as he went along, others, were read by him from library books. One of his favourite authors, and one who became mine was the American, Jack London, who wrote *The Call of the Wild* and other famous adventure stories – tales of dogs and wolves, and of big strong men who faced hazardous journeys through blizzards and over mountains, in search of gold, or animal furs; and others who suffered equal hardships at sea, in search of whales. As a teenager and reading his books myself, I found his stories spiritually transporting me from the stark romance of the Klondyke to the breathtaking perils of storm-tossed seas. It came as no surprise to me when I learned that Jack London himself had experienced the trials of gold prospector, sailor before the mast, and hobo! And I was to find that it was Jack's latter exploit, life on the road, which endeared him to the hearts of the tramps whom I met during my endless travelling round the British Isles. Mind you, despite my admiration for one who had greatly influenced me through his works, I came to realise through time, that there were numerous contradictions in his character; weaknesses that were probably sown and nourished in his childhood by his mother, who suffered from illusions of Anglo-Saxon superiority, and later, when he became influenced by writers like Nietzche and Kipling. Surprisingly, most of my fellow tramps would not admit to any contradictions in the character of their favourite author. He was unique in everything he ever attempted during his short life, according to them.

On 16th September 1985, I boarded a British Airways Jet, for the nine-hour non-stop flight from London, Heathrow, to San Francisco. On arrival, imagine my surprise on reaching the Visitors Reception Area, and observing Stuart Kandell, my host: holding up a banner which read: SAN FRANCISCO – WELCOMES A GEORDIE.

I said to him, "I feel like the Ambassador for Geordieland."

It was a wonderful reception. I could observe the other people around looking at me curiously: pondering who on earth I could be.

On arriving at his home in Oakland, I observed another banner, stretched across his front porch: "America Welcomes Callaghan." So I stood under it, and had my first photo taken in the U.S.A. In the evening I was introduced to Sherry, his fiance, a pretty looking girl, who had just arrived from the animal clinic where she worked as a veterinary surgeon. The three of us went out to lunch in a restaurant beside Oakland Bay; and talked to our hearts' content. Despite the lovely evening we spent, I was pleased when bedtime arrived, the long journey had sapped my energy. I had no sooner got into my bed, when I was joined by their large ginger cat – who apparently desired to share my pillow; after the third time of placing it down by my feet, it suddenly realised I was determined it was getting no opportunity to smother me as I slept. From that night on, it adopted me, no doubt because it sensed I was a cat lover, and it recognised I could converse with it in cat language; and also understand its moods of dependence.

That first night, I slept soundly for thirteen hours; and awoke free from that modern-day disease known as jet-lag. By the time I had finished my breakfast, Stuart had returned from theatre rehearsals; and as planned we set off to visit San Francisco, by means of Bart, the underground railway. On ascending to the surface in the centre of the city, I observed we were at the city terminus of the Cable Car Transport. All around us were buskers, food and drink vendors, and hot gospellers armed with microphones, seemingly determined that no one within reasonable distance should miss hearing their message of Hope and Glory through the means of their particular church! On the corner of the main thoroughfare were two gun-toting, gum-chewing policemen, wearing dark glasses. To me, the whole panorama reminded me of one of the many Hollywood film scenes I had often seen when I was young, and a regular cinema-goer. From a nearby ticket machine we purchased our fares and boarded a cable car, which took us to the Bay Area of the city. For the next two hours or so, with Stuart as my guide, we explored the old sailing ships, the type of vessels that had taken Jack London and other prospectors to the Yukon, in quest of gold; and in an earlier adventure, as a sailor before the mast, the seventeen-year-old Jack London had sailed away to far-off Siberian waters to hunt for whales! From one of the ships, I peered over towards Alcatraz Island, the one-time prison that had housed dangerous criminals but was now a tourist attraction. Jack London, in his writings on social questions, had strongly called for more humane conditions in prisons; never having forgotten his own three month sentence as a result of being arrested on a charge of vagrancy; he claimed the sights he had witnessed inside the prison resulted in him having nightmares for a very long period.

Situated on the balcony of Pier 39 stands the larger than life effigy of Joshua Morton, self-proclaimed Emperor of California. This unusual character, an Englishman who had made his fortune in real-estate in San Francisco during the heydays of the Californian gold-craze, suddenly became bankrupt, and consequently mad. Thereafter, he believed he was Emperor of the United States, Mexico and China! The majority of the citizens of San Francisco, loving his remarkable eccentricity, provided him with a suitable uniform, and living expenses of 30 dollars a month; and they openly accepted his illusions. When he died, about 100,000 people attended his funeral.

On leaving the Bay, we went up on to Nob Hill, the area of the city where the palaces of the wealthy pioneers of the gold-strike of 1849, had stood! Here, only a few hours after the earthquake of 1906, which almost devastated the city, Jack London had sat in the company of the downtrodden: the blacks, the Chinese and Japanese, the despised workers of the city; the latter silently brooding at the loss of their jobs, and their slum shelters; whilst Jack's fertile mind was recording the terrible scenes which one day would result in stories that would increase his growing literary reputation.

Back on Market Street, Stuart took me on a tour of the city. I doubt whether there is another metropolis like San Francisco: here I discovered each ethnic group of people have their own distinctive neighbourhood, complete with housing, community offices, banks, restaurants, and shopping precincts, protected by their own private, armed police.

Even the gay people have consolidated their position in the city and created their own area! Situated on some wasteland, there is a dismal-looking shanty town. The entrance to this makeshift neighbourhood is secured by a huge wooden gateway, over which is a large sign proclaiming: 'People's Park'. Here live the down and out, and the beatniks. I could only presume the city authorities allowed the site to exist either owing to tolerance on their part, or as a preventative measure to discourage the homeless ones from dossing around in doorways and alleyways, and parks as they do in London, and other cities all over the globe.

In the evening, we travelled down town to Jack London Square, which overlooks Oakland Bay! I stood fascinated outside the world famous: FIRST AND LAST CHANCE SALOON, a timber construction, where the young Jack London, at the age of sixteen, had often stood drinking shoulder to shoulder with roughnecks of every description and every nationality, during his lawless, and dangerous, Oyster Pirate days. In front of the building, stands the log cabin which had been transported from Dawson City, in the Yukon; and in which Jack had spent the winter along with other prospectors during the 1896, gold rush. The one-room Saloon, was lavishly decorated with photos and other memorabilia of Oakland's most honoured son. As soon as we entered, Stuart introduced me to the Governor, the grandson of Johnny Heinold, first owner of the Saloon; who had befriended the young

Jack London. I sensed the governor had known beforehand of my intended visit. This was reinforced in my mind, when suddenly one of the customers began playing the tune 'The Keel Row' on what to me, appeared to be a Northumbrian bagpipe! I spent an interesting evening chatting with everyone about the author who had so influenced me. And later, I thanked Stuart; the man who was making all my dreams come true, in Jack London country.

The next morning, I was taken to the theatre in Berkeley and introduced to Stuart's group of actors, and to their resident playwright, Linda Spector; who apart from her literary talents is pretty! The remarkable factor about these actors, apart from their acting skills, is that they are all middle-aged. An experiment, which Stuart had begun at the beginning of his career; which proved so successful, that he continues to teach older would-be actors; and the results are deservedly good notices wherever they perform. After having seen them perform a few brief sketches from one of their current productions; I gave a talk on The Tramp, and Jack London.

The following day was spent exploring, Point Reyes National Park, in the company of Stuart, and one of the actors. I reckon it would take days on end on foot to cover only part of this vast forest with its towering Redwoods. We took a path that leads to Drakes Beach; this part of the coast reminded Francis Drake, of the White Cliffs of the English Coast. Where we sat down for lunch, there could be no doubt in my mind that it was the same place that members of Drake's crew had landed in search of fresh water and food. The only drawback of this beautiful scene, for me, was the heat; palefaces from Geordieland are not accustomed to 90 degrees in the shade. When we arrived back at the Visitors Centre, we learned there had been a serious earthquake in Mexico. In the evening, Sherry, Stuart and I witnessed on television the dreadful devastation in Mexico City. I slept very little that night; my dreams were shattered by visions of the carnage that mother nature had decided to dish out. And to think that Man continuously attempts to outdo nature in the line of destruction!

On the Friday morning, I gave another talk. This time on my childhood, and my writing. After lunch Stuart led me to Oakland City Library, and introduced me to the Librarian in charge of the Jack London Archives. In a secluded nook at a desk, I sat down determined to study the particular kind of magazine stories and press cuttings which I had always failed to get my hands on in the public libraries during my endless travels round the British Isles. At the end of three hours, I had gained a much further insight into the life of this great writer; and discovered he was more of a complex character than I had previously realised. His attitude towards his first wife and two daughters, for instance, really puzzled me!

When I was once more joined in company with the librarian and Stuart, I could sense I was in for yet another surprise; one which had to be the pinnacle of my visit to California! Smilingly, they informed me that a meeting had been arranged for me to visit Glen Ellen, and have a talk with Becky, Jack London's only surviving daughter, then visit the Jack London ranch afterwards! This man can move mountains, thought I, as I thanked them both warmly.

After a late breakfast, Sherry, Stuart and I travelled by car to the Jack London Bookstore in Glen Ellen, which is owned by the author Russ Kingman, whose biography of Jack was well acclaimed. On our arrival, we learned that Becky, a keen soccer fan, was watching her favourite team play, so we altered our timetable, and went up to the ranch! The first thing I did was to go to the graveside of Jack London, and pay homage to the man, who had lived many adventurous lives, yet died tragically at the early age of forty in 1916. His ashes lay buried beneath a huge boulder, taken from the ruins of the nearby Wolf House, a mansion which Jack had claimed would stand for a thousand years! And on observing the magnificent ruins of this edifice, I had no doubt it would have withstood centuries of time. No earthquake would have shattered the Wolf House, only a mysterious fire on the very evening it had been completed gutted its interior, leaving the rugged exterior of a unique ruin that by appearance could very well have been standing for centuries. It is a picturesque monument, which stands as a symbol of the man who built it, and which was probably meant to represent his dreams. Half-a-mile away, stands another formidable mansion, a lesser Wolf House, built by Charmaine, his second wife, in memory of Jack, and which now is a museum stocked with his complete works and recreated writing den.

Climbing up into the hills, and standing beside the lake that Jack had created to serve for irrigation, and often used as a swimming pool, we looked all around us, down to the Valley of the Moon, once a sacred place for the Red Indian Tribes before the White Man arrived and forced them to move on! All this territory had been Jack's own Shangri-La, which earned him deep suspicion and criticism from his former socialist comrades. They appeared to overlook the full employment Jack provided for so many hands, all receiving good wages and living accommodation. Becoming a wealthy landowner, yet practising socialist principles towards his workforce, was just one of Jack's contradictions.

A little after 4.30 in the afternoon, we were closeted comfortably in a back room of the bookshop; and as soon as the recording equipment was set up, I began my talk with Becky, Jack London's daughter.

I began by stating that I had been a fervent admirer of her father's work since I was a lad but that until I was a young man, I had been under the impression that he was solely a writer of fiction. Until one cold winter's evening, when being down-and-out in London, I had entered a public library in order to be warm; it was then I had come across her father's book *People of the Abyss*, his indictment of the terrible living conditions in the East End of London.

Becky said, "My father straightened out the false views held, that London was a den of criminality. He pointed out that the area was downgraded due to unemployment and poverty." I then commented that it was whilst I was tramping around my own country that I also came across her father's writings on hoboes, and vagrancy.

She replied, "When my sister Joan and I were children, our father often took us to San Francisco for the day. As we walked up Market Street, my father would often be met by hoboes, and he would give handouts. My father knew these people were rejected by society; he had experienced it, and never forgot it. His road life was his school of learning." I mentioned I had seen two films in my time, adapted from stories of her father; one being *The Call of the Wild*.

Becky said, "Daddy, didn't get much royalties on the earlier films made during his lifetime – most of the film-makers spoiled his stories. They made his *Call of the Wild* into a love story; which was really a dog story."

I remarked that her father's book *John Barleycorn* had been a favourite read of all the tramps I had come across and who were readers of his work. I never mentioned the reason why my brother tramps had looked upon this particular book with so much favour. They had expressed pride that Jack London could hold his liquor, yet remain master of it. It was an opinion I could not share! My reading and study of *John Barleycorn* led me to the conclusion that it was a sad testimony of a great writer who had become a victim of self-delusion, in claiming he had conquered alcohol, that he had no need of it, and only drank for social reasons.

Becky said, "Daddy, would sooner have a bag of candy; he only drank when he was attracted to it by company. Alcohol was not necessary to him. Whenever he took me and Joan out to lunch, he always had coffee."

Further on in our talk, Becky explained why her father and mother, Jack's first wife, had parted, whilst she and sister Joan were quite young.

"He wished to travel round, without planning. Mother was a home-planner; that is why mother and he never got on together."

Glancing over to a shelf, where could be seen some of Jack London's books, she smiled and said quite proudly: "Daddy is my favourite author. Next is Charles Dickens. Both authors, who can be read and read again."

Finally, she got to talking about her sister Joan and how she had been active in union work, and became Treasurer of the Pacific Coast of San Francisco Farm Workers' Union, wrote articles for the union movement; and wrote a biography of her father. I told Becky I had read it.

Finally, Becky said: "You know what! I am the only person alive today who has talked to daddy face-to-face. I sometimes can't accept he's gone; I feel as though I'm expecting him to enter the room anytime!"

For a full hour we had covered all important aspects of her father's life; what had impressed me about Jack London's daughter, was her entire devotion to the memory of her father; no mention of his failings; no criticism about his deliberate act of leaving his whole estate to Charmaine, his second wife; not one dollar apiece did Jack's first wife, and his two daughters receive from the future royalties, which were to be earned on his books and film-rights. I find it hard to fathom, in a man who otherwise was the most generous of human beings! Before we left Glen Ellen, Stuart took a number of snaps of Becky and myself outside, in front of the Jack London Bookstore.

We were having breakfast the following morning, when Stuart enquired, "Tell me Tom, have you read any of John Steinbeck's work?" I was at that moment wondering what we intended doing for the day, considering he had remained away from the theatre, and had been on the phone for at least ten minutes, during which I had heard my name being mentioned.

In answer to his question I replied, "*The Grapes of Wrath* was Steinbeck's first book I ever read," wondering what was behind the sudden interest in this author! Then he asked me whether I had read *Cannery Row*? Yes I had, another great book of his. And I was surprised to learn, later, that the main character, 'Doc' Ricketts, who had his marine laboratory on Cannery Row, was authentic; and that Steinbeck himself often worked along with the 'Doc' in his laboratory on Cannery Row!

"Well, Tom," he began smilingly, "I'm going to take you to Monterey, to meet my brother and his wife; and this evening we'll visit Cannery Row – How does that suit you?"

"It suits me find, Sir. Just get out your magic carpet – and I'll be ready!" said I rubbing my hands with glee.

Stuart's brother and his wife, were running a motel, on the outskirts of Monterey. And like all the other people I had been introduced to since my arrival in California, I found them to be warm friendly folks. After a meal, Stuart and his brother and I motored down to Cannery Row. The street lights were just coming on as we were about to enter the Row. For a moment we stood to admire the bronze bust of John

Steinbeck on its pedestal, the man who through his unforgettable stories of the characters of the Old Cannery Row put the street on the map; and now made it the most popular tourist attraction in Monterey. As we took our leisurely walk along the mile-long street, the scene was just about what I had imagined it would be, as described in the stories of Cannery Row; despite that none of the old canneries and reduction-plants were now in business. Externally, the architecture was the same; internally the old canneries had been converted into shops and restaurants. Wisely, the planner had completely left the original marine laboratory of 'Doc' Edward Ricketts, even though it was now serving the purpose of a private club. After a couple of beers we made our way back to the car; and so I said goodbye to the Row, and to the ghosts of Steinbeck, and 'Doc' Ricketts; I had closeted another nostalgic moment which I could store into my memory library, to be drawn upon in time to come.

Next morning, after breakfast, we bid our hosts a fond farewell; and drove into Monterey. This small town is typical of the Spanish influence which was prominent in this part of Mexican California, before its annexation by the U.S.A. As we stood in the town square, I said to Stuart, "This place reminds me of the film *South of the Border*, starring Gene Autrey."

The fine-looking building in front of us, and known as Colton Hall, was where California's Constitution was written in 1849. Stuart smilingly replied, "Okay, let's look inside, we may find Gene Autrey waiting to welcome us!"

Upstairs in the main room, the scene was that of a recess in the Convention of 1849: papers and books, official documents and pens and ink bottles were spread out on the tables. You almost felt like that any moment the generals and the administrators would suddenly return – barging into the room, and possibly demand our arrest on the suspicion of being spies! Were it so in reality, we wouldn't have far to travel to our place of confinement; the jail-house was situated on the ground floor at the rear of the building. And a forbidding-looking gaol it appeared, with its narrow cells, bare stone floors, thick granite walls and strong barred doors and windows. It was a typical jail of the type I had witnessed in many a Western film, the one conspicuous object in each of these cells, which made the picture more realistic than the film jailhouse, was the chamber pot..

When we arrived back in Oakland at teatime, Sherry was at home having finished work at the animal clinic earlier, on account of it being the occasion of the Jewish New Year. And to my delight, I was invited to accompany them to the Synagogue, in Berkeley. Though I am not religious myself, I am sincerely curious as to how different Churches hold their respective services. When I was a lad, it had been my custom to attend Sunday School classes of all the various churches in my neighbourhood. My favourite brand of religious service had always been the Salvation Army; apart from the sentiment that my mother had been a Salvationist before she married; I love their melodious hymns – which sound a little like Country and Western music!

Back home, Stuart reminded me of my proposed busking stint, which I intended doing the following day, in the company of, Paul, a professional busker; Stuart and Sherry would be at the Synagogue most of the day.

By eleven o'clock the following morning, Paul and I were on the main thoroughfare in San Francisco, the first of his three regular pitches in the city, and ready to commence our performance. Paul played the flute, and was no mean musician; I played no musical instrument, my busking talent resided in my vocal chords; I've always had a good singing voice, especially when I was young, but in between my singing, Paul suggested I play the tambourine – which he had brought along; I blessed my past experience in having observed the Salvation Army lasses!

After a while, and for the sake of novelty, I decided to sing a Geordie song, *Cushy Butterfield* and in Geordie dialect! The moment I began singing it, passers by stopped in their tracks, their faces registering amusement; curiosity or downright bafflement. On completing the song, the onlookers smiled in amazement, with the exception of one middle-aged gentleman, who still appeared uncertain as to what language I had been singing in. He approached me, and kindly enquired what part of the world I hailed from?

"I am a Geordie, Sir."

And before I could elaborate, he remarked: "Ah! From Russia! Pleased to have met you." And placing a contribution into the hat he strode off briskly. I glanced at Paul and shrugged my shoulders in amusement and said:

"That is the first time I have been taken to be a Russian; I've often been mistaken for a Welshman, Irishman, or Scotsman; but never a Russian; I must tell my socialist friends back home in England."

Paul replied: "To be honest, the dialect, had me puzzled; you could very well have been a Russian, for my money!" Well, that was my last song in Geordie lingo; but it had created curiosity and an audience, and no busker complains about that.

Paul's next pitch was in the Japanese area of the city, his favourite location. Here, he always concentrated on Japanese music; and so I had to keep with the tambourine, doing my utmost to keep in tune with Paul's playing of the flute, for I was a stranger to such music. In the afternoon, I treated him to lunch in one of the local restaurants; I enjoyed the food, though Japanese beer did not encourage my taste buds.

At the end of our working day, Paul decided to remain in San Francisco for a few hours longer; and I boarded the Underground back to Oakland! When I entered the candle-lit dining room, I observed the snow-white table cloth covering the dining table on which was spread the traditional Jewish New Year Feast; strange but delicious food, and three kinds of wine; and places set for three! I thought to myself: What a lucky fellow I am, to be an invited guest to such a feast and by two such nice people.

It was an occasion I would not forget: good company, good food and good wine. And so off to bed, with the cat resting at my feet.

By the time I arose next morning, Sherry had gone to the clinic, and Stuart to the theatre. After my breakfast, I went down town on a previously arranged visit to the Creative Growth Centre, on 24th Street, Oakland. This particular centre in Oakland is an organisation, one of the few, unfortunately, whether in America, Britain or elsewhere, which is dedicated to the exploring of the artistic potential of adults who are severely handicapped, mentally, physically, or emotionally. For two hours, I moved round the Centre, looking at and examining all possible kinds of art: sculpture, pottery, painting, woodwork and so on, and talking with the artists able to communicate verbally. The simple beauty of all this artistic creation was that these disabled artists were creating what appealed to them! Many of them were not aware of the difference between good and bad art, therefore there was no form of snobbery or foolish criticism of each other's work, no intellectual barrier existed between them. Those individuals, who showed promise, were given the opportunity to prove whether they can perhaps make a living with their work. The others, well they were proving they were not armchair zombies after all! For most of these unfortunate people had until recently been incarcerated inside institutions, for years on end without any creative pastimes, not even the use of pencil and paper! During my years of nursing in mental institutions, I had observed, daily, such wasted lives, often with sad dismay and frustration, because I alone couldn't improve their lot.

On leaving the Centre, I went on a walk around Oakland, looking at the various locations where Jack London had lived as a boy, as a teenager, and during his early days of marriage to Bess, his fist wife. I went back to 3929 Everett Avenue, and tea, feeling satisfied at having covered another bit of the Jack London trail.

The following morning, Friday, we loaded up the boot of the car with camping gear and backpacks, and set off towards the High Sierras, still on the trail! The young Jack London had travelled over the same mountains on foot; but then we too were determined to explore some of the territory on foot. Indeed, it turned out later, we had to cover more ground on foot than we had planned! When we got as far as Yosemite Creek camping site, we staked our claim to one of the vacant plots, before continuing our journey down to Yosemite Valley.

The Valley is surrounded by sheer vertical cliffs that rise up, seemingly to the heavens, and giant trees which were old at the time of the very early Indian inhabitants of the Valley; and the fantastic waterfalls plunging down from the mountains, which serve to supply the lakes in the valley basin, are a sight I shall never forget. Beautiful natural landscapes always affect me; I feel as though I belong in their midst! When I was a young man, I could not keep away from the English Lakes and their mountains surrounding them; and though I would be inevitably broke during such times, by the means of casual work I was always able to prolong my stay.

The forest walks that surround the valley basin are alive with wildlife; chipmunks, deer, squirrels, and birds of all description – and colour. The bears apparently appear during the night, seeking food that perhaps some campers have failed to store away in the boot of their car despite Federal Notices urging them to do so! One hears of some campers who have had their car wrecked during the night, because they had left food visibly on view on the back seats of their car. Bears have no respect for man or his automobile, when it comes to the grabbing of some tasty grub. And of course the feeding of wildlife is strictly forbidden.

Our final exploration before returning up the mountain to our camp, was to the Indian Village, a tourist attraction only – the Indians are now housed on modern reservations. Whether they are happier in possessing modern conveniences, rather than being on their former happy hunting grounds in Yosemite Valley, where their roots really are, only they themselves could answer. Myself, I doubt it.

There are about a dozen sites at Yosemite Creek, for campers, each with a fireplace, and space for a car, and a tent. The toilet block provided cold water only; but then what fool expects to be provided with running hot water, up in the mountains? Certainly not Stuart, or myself, both keen outdoor men. There was one aspect of his outdoor fascination which I had never taken to: mountain climbing! I suggested to him that there were sufficient worthwhile risks in hill walking, and sleeping rough no matter what the weather, without the added risk of breaking one's neck in the scaling of mountain sides. I had witnessed mountaineers at work during my tramping journeys through the wilderness of North Wales, and I had always assured myself that I would sooner risk meeting a bad tempered ghost, in any of the cemeteries I often kipped in on a night, than attempt to scale impossible heights. But Stuart laughed off my fears; he was an amazingly daring character – certainly a man to face danger with. As we prepared to kip down, we heard the distant call of some wolf, soon responded to by another from a different location. I said to Stuart: "There goes Jack London's Call of the Wild!"

Silence, once more. In a short space of time I was slipping away into never-never land. The only disturbance during the night, was the sound of thunder – followed by a swift but brief downpour.

Next morning, we shaved, had breakfast, then cleaned up our site and ensured the fire was completely dead; then drove off to our next camping site. On arriving there, we got out our backpacks, secured the car, and set off up the mountain towards the Ranger Station, to call on a friend of Stuart's. What surprised me on entering the two-room log cabin of the Rangers, was to discover that his friend, the Ranger on duty, was a pretty young woman, dressed like one of those Canadian Mountain Police I had often seen in the films; she reminded me of Jeanette McDonald. In the middle of the office-cum-living room, was a large pot-belly stove, which served to heat the cabin and to cook upon. After we exchanged greetings, she poured out three mugs of coffee from the pot that had been resting on top of the stove! The brew was so strong I had to saturate it with the rough brown sugar she gave me; she and Stuart drank theirs without sugar – I shuddered at the thought of it, thinking that if all Mountain Rangers and Cowboys drank such coffee as their usual beverage, they had no need of alcohol.

We remained in her company for an hour having a good discussion and a laugh. On leaving, she told us to look in on our way back down the mountain, so as she would know we were safe and well! On our arriving at Tioga Pass, elevation 9945ft, we stood looking up and ahead at the snow-capped peaks shimmering in the morning sun. Surprisingly, considering how high we were up in the mountains, it was reasonably warm. The view towards the Valley presented another fantastic landscape – for a moment, I imagined I was Ronald Coleman, exhilarated at the vision of Shangri-La, apparently concealed in this amazing mountain kingdom! I thought that such majestic scenes of spiritual-serenity were as near to a heaven as I would ever experience; or anyone else for that matter. I was at peace, as I always am in such surroundings! And may the industrial and commercial speculators never get the opportunity to rape such peaceful kingdoms in their never ceasing scramble for profit under the guise of progress.

It was almost with sorrow that with the approach of evening, we began our descent to our camp, paying another call on the way at the Ranger Station. This time I resisted the offer of coffee, and instead accepted a glass of clear mountain spring water which was delicious.

The following afternoon we set off over the mountain passes en route to June

Lake, to stay the night with a friend of Stuart's. I was becoming amazed at the number of his friends who all lived in lovely locations. June Lake, I discovered to be a small village of Alpine-design cottages, and chalet-type villas, situated round one end of the lake. Stuart informed me that during winter time the village is completely cut off from the outside world; those who resided all the year round must stock up with food and logs for their all-purpose stoves.

Stuart's friend, Honey; made me most welcome, and from the beginning proved to have a good sense of humour. Within an hour of being in her company I sensed she was the type of pioneer woman who was capable of facing life under any circumstances; the kind of woman that Jack London described, who uncomplainingly followed their menfolk from one goldfield to another, and made their lives as normal as possible under the most difficult of hardships. Honey was in her early fifties, young in appearance, and her fine clear skin was that of a twenty-year-old girl; and her figure was still trim; no doubt she had looked after herself, despite the hard work entailed during winter, sawing logs and clearing snow daily.

When she took me up to the guest room where I would be sleeping that night, I observed her dog following us. Honey remarked to me: "If you're wondering why the dog tags along, Tom, it's because she sleeps in the guest room, where I'm putting you."

Said I: "I'm sure she'll sense I'm an animal lover, so we'll get along all right," hoping the creature didn't talk or snore in her sleep.

During the night when I rose to visit the bathroom, the dog rose too and followed me, remaining outside until I came out and back to the bedroom; nor did it lie down again until I was back in bed. This canine house guard was taking no chances that the stranger, who spoke in a strange dialect, might attempt to abscond during the night. Next morning after breakfast and a walk round the lake, we bid Honey a fond farewell. As we drove off, Stuart said, "Well, Tom, I'm taking you to Bodie! A one-time gold-rush town, to give you an impression of the environment Jack London would have faced when he arrived in Dawson City, in the Klondyke."

From Highway 167, we drove down Cottonwood Canyon, the last three miles of our journey down the original rough dirt road on which the old stagecoaches had travelled all those years ago, when Bodie, was in full swing.

At the head of the Canyon Stuart pulled up, and we got out of the car! The sight below thrilled me no end. I could hardly believe my senses; I was actually looking down on to a typical Cowboy town, the like of which I had often seen on the silver screen, many a Saturday afternoon, when I was a kid. There was the main street, consisting mainly of saloons and boarding houses, surrounded by groups of miners' cabins, the bank, hotels, sheriff's office, and jailhouse, and the now disused mining works. Coming along the main street on his horse, I could make out the Resident Ranger, dressed for all the world like my favourite boyhood Cowboy, Tom Mix.

"This is fantastic," said I, looking at Stuart. "And I have you to thank for my trip of a lifetime."

He smiled before remarking, "It's a pleasure. After all, I look upon you as the Jack London of Benwell."

We walked down into the town. On our left was the town cemetery, where I learned the respectable citizens of Bodie were buried; outside it, and unfenced, was 'Boot Hill'! Here, the bad men, and the prostitutes lay buried side by side. At that moment the Ranger rode by, greeting us as he did so. I said to Stuart, "I wouldn't have minded being a Ranger here when I was younger. Having a whole ghost town to myself, once the day's last visitor had departed."

"Not quite!" Stuart explained, "During the summer season, a few of the tourists camp out in the hills above the town, so the Ranger will have to patrol in the evenings to ensure no bad guy damages any of the buildings."

For the next three hours we walked round the town, exploring almost every building, and some of them really were ghostlike in some sense! The saloons were still equipped with most of their fittings, and tables and chairs – with playing cards lying around. On the bar shelves were numbers of cobwebbed empty bottles. Similar scenes were to be seen in other buildings – stores, hotels and boarding houses, where large items of furniture and bellystoves had been left behind by the sudden departure of the town's population at the news that another gold-strike was taking place elsewhere in the region, or over the nearby border in Nevada. Because of the lack of adequate transport, miners and their families, and trade proprietors, simply left large cumbersome items of furniture behind. It was a ghost town in every sense of the word. Even the bunks and chamber pots remained in the jailhouse. I was surprised to learn, that during the gold fever of 1879, the population of Bodie had been almost 10,000 people. And the four busiest trades of all, apart from the mining of gold, were the saloons, the prostitutes, the undertakers, and the Sheriff's Office.

The town of Bodie was named after Bill Bodey, one of the four wandering prospectors who first discovered gold in the surrounding hills, in the Fall of 1859! Bill Bodey died in a snowstorm in the same winter. It was twenty years later that his body was removed from the location where he had collapsed and died in the snow, and reburied in the Camp Cemetery. And the town was then named Bodie (misspelled) in his honour.

One of the most famous prostitutes was Rosa May, an Irish girl, with the reputation for a heart of gold. Many a miner was helped by her generosity, and she was known to be very fond of children. Rosa May died in her thirties, after nursing sick miners during the pneumonia epidemic of 1912. Yet, despite her sacrifice, her Christian townsfolk refused her burial in consecrated ground! As I stood within the cabin where she had lived, in the red-light district, situated behind the main street, I silently paid tribute to her memory. I learned later, that a well known American author, had attended to her grave, and erected fencing around it. More power to his pen; I salute him.

After Stuart had taken a number of snaps of me at various locations in the town, it was time to move on. Back on to Highway 167, and the mountain trails again. We had got as far as pass White Wolf, when suddenly the car engine stalled, then packed up altogether. I remained in the car whilst Stuart walked ahead to a service point to phone for assistance. By the time the breakdown truck arrived, and hauled us down to Yosemite, where we learned the car would have to be left behind, it was too late to move further, so we camped for the night at Yosemite.

Next morning after breakfast, we left the Valley, and took to the trail with our backpacks, hoping to hitchhike to San Francisco at least. After our fourth and last lift of the day, we arrived in Oakland soon after seven in the evening.

The following afternoon I spent on my own exploring more of the boyhood haunts of Jack London. I got talking to a policeman; surprisingly, he too was an admirer of the author! Having taken me for an Irishman, I decided not to refute him; with a surname like mine he wouldn't have believed me; and I doubted whether he could have discriminated between my Geordie dialect, and the speech, spoken by the Irish of Northern Ireland.

"Did you know that Jack London's real father, was an Irishman?" he enquired.

"I did," said I. "He was self-styled Professor Chaney. And quite a clever chap by all the accounts I've read of him."

"It puzzles me why Chaney denied paternal responsibility for his son," remarked the Policeman. "After all," he continued, "Chaney was always hard up; and his son became famous; and he was always generous. It surely would have done Chaney a lot of good to admit he was Jack's father!"

Said I in reply: "It proves one thing – Chaney wasn't a guy looking for a hand-out. And of course Jack was a young man afore he ever heard of Chaney being his father. No doubt too late to make-up, as far as his father was concerned."

After further discussion on our favourite author, we bid each other good day; and I continued my exploration of Jack London territory. On the Friday evening, Stuart and Sherry held a champagne party at home, and the whole cast of the Stagebridge Theatre were present! Stuart had photocopied a number of Tyneside songs from a book I had brought from Newcastle; it was great to hear them all singing such numbers as *Cushy Butterfield, The Keelrow, Keep Your Feet Still Geordie Hinny,* and others. They were all a grand lot of folks! Indeed everyone I had met during my stay in California, whether by being introduced to them by my hosts, or coming across them on the city streets during my walks, were polite and eager to be helpful to a stranger. In other words, I was pleased to learn that my life-long views, that ordinary people no matter where they reside, are nice folks, had been substantiated.

During the next couple of days, Stuart introduced me to a number of authors at different venues; and I found our talks very interesting and helpful! Before meeting these American writers, I had met with five well-known writers in my own country: the late Angela Carter; and the playwright Cecil Taylor, in whose profitable company I had spent a week in the spring of 1978, in the Lake District, under the auspices of Northern Arts. Then the late Sid Chaplin, who had written the introduction to my first book. Followed by Bruce Allsopp, then Frank Graham. I am indebted to them all for their very sound advice.

Sadly, my Jack London Pilgrimage came to an end; and on the Monday I boarded my plane from San Francisco to Heathrow. It had been a wonderful experience, all thanks to my generous hosts.

The following year, Stuart and Sherry were married. And now they have two young beautiful daughters: Sophia Lianna, and Arianna Fay, who have adopted me as their Uncle.

In the spring of 1988, I once more took to the road for three months. Would the wanderlust, ever leave me be? Not according to the poet Robert W. Service!

> Wild heart, child heart, all of the world your home.
> Glad heart, mad heart, what can you do but roam?
> Oh, I'll beat it once more in the morning boys,
> With a pinch of tea and a crust;
> For you cannot deny
> When you hark to the cry
> Of the Wan-der-lust.

The Wanderlust, Robert W. Service